Cambridge Elements ☰

Elements in the Economics of Emerging Markets
edited by
Bruno S. Sergi
Harvard University

CAN BRICS DE-DOLLARIZE THE GLOBAL FINANCIAL SYSTEM?

Zongyuan Zoe Liu
Tufts University

Mihaela Papa
Tufts University

CAMBRIDGE
UNIVERSITY PRESS

University Printing House, Cambridge CB2 8BS, United Kingdom

One Liberty Plaza, 20th Floor, New York, NY 10006, USA

477 Williamstown Road, Port Melbourne, VIC 3207, Australia

314–321, 3rd Floor, Plot 3, Splendor Forum, Jasola District Centre,
New Delhi – 110025, India

103 Penang Road, #05–06/07, Visioncrest Commercial, Singapore 238467

Cambridge University Press is part of the University of Cambridge.

It furthers the University's mission by disseminating knowledge in the pursuit of
education, learning, and research at the highest international levels of excellence.

www.cambridge.org
Information on this title: www.cambridge.org/9781009014625
DOI: 10.1017/9781009029544

First published 2022

A catalogue record for this publication is available from the British Library.

ISBN 978-1-009-01462-5 Paperback
ISSN 2631-8598 (online)
ISSN 2631-858X (print)

Can BRICS De-dollarize the Global Financial System?

Elements in the Economics of Emerging Markets

DOI: 10.1017/9781009029544
First published online: February 2022

Zongyuan Zoe Liu
Tufts University

Mihaela Papa
Tufts University

Author for correspondence: Zongyuan Zoe Liu, zliu@cfr.org

Abstract: Existing scholarship has not systematically examined BRICS (Brazil, Russia, India, China, South Africa) as a rising power de-dollarization coalition despite the group developing multiple de-dollarization initiatives to reduce currency risk and bypass US sanctions. To fill this gap, this study develops a "Pathways to De-dollarization" framework and applies it to analyze the institutional and market mechanisms that BRICS countries have created at the BRICS, sub-BRICS, and BRICS Plus levels. This framework identifies the leaders and followers of the BRICS de-dollarization coalition, assesses its robustness, and discerns how BRICS mobilizes other stakeholders. The authors employ process tracing, content analysis, semi-structured interviews, archival research, and statistical analysis of quantitative market data to analyze BRICS activities during 2009–2021. They find that BRICS' coalitional de-dollarization initiatives have established critical infrastructure for a prospective alternative nondollar global financial system. This title is also available as Open Access on Cambridge Core.

Keywords: global financial governance, BRICS, de-dollarization, currency power, emerging economies

ISBNs: 9781009014625 (PB), 9781009029544 (OC)
ISSNs: 2631-8598 (online), 2631-858X (print)

Contents

1 Introduction

The US dollar's supremacy and US global leadership have been increasingly questioned since the 2007–2008 global financial crisis. The fact that this crisis originated in the United States raised concerns about the reliability of US leadership and the rationality of preserving the dollar's hegemonic position in the global financial system. This crisis also created an opportunity for rising powers to seek greater status and representation in global governance. In 2009, Russian President Dmitry Medvedev (2009) hosted the first BRIC (Brazil, Russia, India, China) Summit in Yekaterinburg to explore how to "overcome the crisis and establish a fairer international system ... and discuss the parameters for a new financial system." Since South Africa joined BRIC in 2010, transforming BRIC into BRICS, the five members have achieved policy coordination in over seventy issue areas (Kirton and Larionova, 2018; Brazil MFA, 2020). BRICS' foremost achievements have been in the area of financial cooperation, as evidenced by the establishment of the New Development Bank (NDB), the Contingent Reserve Arrangement (CRA), and various other financial coordination mechanisms.

Despite the breadth of the BRICS countries' financial cooperation and their growing interconnectedness, BRICS' activities in the monetary realm have been understudied. Yet the stakes of BRICS' de-dollarization initiatives are particularly high. The US dollar is the dominant currency in the global financial and monetary system and affects various aspects of global affairs. As such, the dollar's power and prestige have been central to American global leadership (see also Helleiner and Kirshner, 2009, p. 1). The NDB's commitment to using local currency finance rather than solely relying on the US dollar is merely the tip of the iceberg of BRICS' de-dollarization initiatives.[1] It is also an open question whether the accelerated de-dollarization process in Russia and China, triggered by their growing tensions with the United States, is only a temporary change, or whether it forms a broader paradigm shift in global finance. To give this some context, the share of the US dollar in Russia–China bilateral trade settlement fell from nearly 90 percent in 2015 to 46 percent in 2020 (Simes, 2020). Moreover, Russia and China have launched their own cross-border payment mechanisms as alternatives to the US-dominated Society for Worldwide Interbank Financial Telecommunication (SWIFT) network. BRICS has also conceptualized a common BRICS Pay system for retail payments and transactions among member countries, which has been enabled by rapid progress in the financial technology (fintech) sector. Such

---

[1] The President of the NDB outlined the bank's mission of promoting the use of local currencies in development finance (Kamath, 2020).

de-dollarization initiatives are happening largely under the radar of contemporary scholarship. Leaders of these initiatives are reform-oriented rising powers, including strategic adversaries of the United States, that have expressed discontent with the existing US-led dollar-based global financial system. Could these empirical cases serve as the "canary in the coal mine" and represent a larger de-dollarization movement?

To systematically examine the nature and impact of these activities, this research seeks to answer a critical question: *Can BRICS de-dollarize the US-led global financial system?* The underlying assumption of this study is that the dominant currency status of the US dollar may not be permanent. The US dollar's displacement of the previous hegemonic currency, namely, the British pound sterling, attests to this notion. The importance of examining BRICS' challenge to the US dollar's dominance lies in the group's collective economic power. BRICS accounts for 24 percent of world GDP and over 16 percent of world trade (BRICS India, 2021). Thus, BRICS' de-dollarization activities would not only impact inter-BRICS financial relations but also create a ripple effect globally. An examination of BRICS' de-dollarization efforts can help answer the broader question of whether rising powers can gain followers and lead change at a global scale. Can de-dollarization champions within BRICS mobilize less interested BRICS members around this agenda? Can they expand their de-dollarization initiatives beyond BRICS and create economies of scale across several platforms that exclude the United States and other major Western powers such as the Shanghai Cooperation Organization (SCO)?

Analyzing BRICS as a de-dollarization coalition and how it could mobilize other actors will contribute new and needed insights to the scholarship on rising powers and their impact on US global leadership. This study examines how the US dollar's dominant position in the global financial system, the very foundation of its global leadership, can be undermined. This topic has important national security implications for the United States. The United States relies upon the dollar's dominant currency status to credibly exercise coercive economic statecraft and sanction its adversaries. An increasingly de-dollarized world would weaken the United States' ability to alter the behavior of its adversaries and could consequently magnify US national security threats.

To investigate whether BRICS can de-dollarize the US-led global financial system, we develop an analytical framework called "Pathways to De-dollarization." This framework explains how a rising power coalition can pursue de-dollarization to challenge the dollar hegemony. It complements existing scholarship on the dominant currency paradigm, currency statecraft, collective financial statecraft, and the political economy of rising power coalitions. Our framework conceptualizes two sets of risk mitigation strategies that rising powers can pursue simultaneously to reduce their rising risk exposure to the dollar's hegemonic power: "go-it-alone" and "reform-the-status-quo." Both enable a rising power coalition, such as BRICS, to pursue de-dollarization as a means of reducing risk exposure to the US dollar and US sanctions. More broadly, these de-dollarization strategies can help the rising power coalition achieve greater financial and geopolitical autonomy and/or increase its global influence. "Go-it-alone" de-dollarization strategies refer to initiatives to establish and govern new nondollar-based institutions and/or market mechanisms. Such measures enable coalition members to diversify currency risks and maintain open access to the global financial system when facing US sanctions. The expansion of these initiatives could lead to the formation of an alternative or parallel system that is independent of the US dollar and rules made by leading Western powers. In contrast, "reform-the-status-quo" initiatives refer to coalitional efforts to renegotiate the rules of the existing system. Such initiatives involve collective bargaining with incumbent powers to dilute the US dollar's dominance. If successful, these reform-oriented initiatives would diversify the representation of currencies in the existing system. Following these two strategies, our framework analyzes institutional and market mechanisms through which a rising power coalition can attempt to de-dollarize the existing global financial system.

This "Pathways to De-dollarization" framework is applied to examine BRICS' de-dollarization activities. By doing so, this study presents the first systematic analysis of de-dollarization initiatives by a rising power coalition. We find that BRICS members have demonstrated an unambiguous consensus and a strong commitment to promoting the use of local currencies in international settlements and building a nondollar alternative global financial infrastructure. They have simultaneously pursued both "go-it-alone" and "reform-the-status-quo" initiatives. For example, BRICS has established the NDB to de-dollarize development finance. The group has also been planning the launch of a common payment framework that can be integrated with a BRICS digital currency to de-dollarize global financial infrastructure. Most de-dollarization initiatives have taken place at the sub-BRICS level. For example, China has successfully launched the yuan oil futures contract, a new financial instrument to de-dollarize the global oil trade. Both China and Russia have developed their own cross-border messaging systems. BRICS has also collectively pursued reformist approaches, such as creating the dollar-based CRA, advocating for the reform of the IMF Special Drawing Rights, and forming a BRICS stock exchanges alliance within the existing system. Together, these initiatives suggest that BRICS has not only attempted to reform the existing system to better incorporate its interests but has also created a nascent de-dollarization infrastructure that supports global de-dollarization in the long term. BRICS' collective efforts to establish an alternative nondollar financial system have the potential to completely immunize participants from both exchange and sanction risks stemming from the dollar's dominance and US hegemonic position. In the long run, the BRICS de-dollarization infrastructure may even serve as the basis for a broader de-dollarization coalition that includes regional organizations. This coalitional de-dollarization infrastructure could be attractive to US allies who seek greater monetary autonomy and to continue trading with countries that are under US sanctions. For example, the Bank of England Governor Mark Carney (2019) told central bankers at the Jackson Hole Symposium that the dollar's dominance is the "destabilizing asymmetry" growing "at the heart of international monetary and financial system." He proposed a new Synthetic Hegemonic Currency possibly provided through a network of central bank digital currencies (Carney, 2019). Similarly, the BRICS countries are in the process of developing a BRICS digital currency called BRICS Coin, which sets the stage for digital de-dollarization.

The emerging BRICS de-dollarization infrastructure does not yet allow the BRICS members to make a complete break from the existing US dollar-based financial system. BRICS de-dollarization initiatives are predominantly happening at the sub-BRICS level and have not achieved the necessary economies of scale to de-dollarize the existing global financial system. There are two major constraints that prevent BRICS from forming a unitary de-dollarization coalition. First, some BRICS members have closer relationships with the United States than with fellow BRICS members. This is evident in the case of India and its relationships with the United States and with China. While this prevents BRICS members from adopting a formal, cohesive de-dollarization strategy in the near term, they may still informally pursue de-dollarization initiatives. Second, some BRICS members, such as Brazil and South Africa, are less vulnerable to US sanctions and have economies that are more integrated into the dollar system than others. Thus, the BRICS members have neither group-level consensus on de-dollarization nor do they share the same sense of urgency to prioritize de-dollarization. All of them are interested in reducing their dependence on the US dollar, but not all want to be separated from the US-led global financial system. Most BRICS members still hold large amounts of US dollar assets in their reserves, so the weakening of the US dollar imposes losses on them.

Existing financial realities cannot be altered in the near term. Moreover, the potential benefits of de-dollarization come at a cost. Breaking away from the existing dollar-based global system and market structure is analogous to self-imposed isolation from the existing system. BRICS would face significant separation costs, with the most immediate ones being increased costs of cross-border transactions, more expensive capital raising in the dollar-based global markets, and reduced competitiveness of their firms in foreign markets due to a shortage of dollar funding. Whether the BRICS governments could credibly enforce de-dollarization initiatives at the firm level, especially on firms operating in foreign territories where the US dollar is the dominant and preferred currency, is questionable. Additionally, the dollar is also global investors' choice of "safe haven" currency during major economic crises. Investors turned to US dollars during the 2007–2008 global financial crisis and the 2020 COVID-19-related economic turmoil, expecting the dollar to hold its value. In both crises, the US Federal Reserve expanded currency swap lines with several other central banks to provide dollar liquidity. A nondollar system would exacerbate issues created by a lack of access to dollar liquidity in times of crises. Such de-dollarization costs deter countries from willingly revolting against the dollar hegemony. Even Russia, a country that is now actively accelerating its de-dollarization process, is not voluntarily pursuing this agenda. As Russian President Putin said, "Russia did not want to give up the dollar as the reserve currency or means of payment, but it was forced to do it" (TASS Russian News Agency, 2021b).

This Element is organized as follows: Section 2 argues that the existing scholarship on currency power, economic statecraft, and BRICS as a coalition lacks a systematic explanation for BRICS coalitional behavior in the de-dollarization space. It introduces a new analytical framework to address this gap. Section 3 traces the emergence of de-dollarization in BRICS cooperation and evaluates BRICS' collective commitment to de-dollarization. Section 4 analyzes BRICS "go-it-alone" initiatives to de-dollarize by establishing new institutions and new markets. Section 5 investigates BRICS' "reform-the-status-quo" initiatives to disrupt the US-led global financial system from the inside. Section 6 presents the findings, discusses the implications of BRICS de-dollarization coalition for US global leadership, and concludes with suggestions for areas of future research.

2 A Coalitional De-dollarization Challenge?

This section discusses the three categories of scholarship that are most relevant for examining how rising powers could pose a coalitional de-dollarization challenge: (1) the international political economy literature on currency power, economic statecraft, and the international monetary system; (2) the international relations literature on rising powers and rising power alliances; and (3) the BRICS studies literature. While these three fields of study offer insights into some aspects of our research question, none of them explicitly addresses the question of rising powers' monetary coalitions, especially BRICS as a de-dollarization coalition. To address this gap, we first introduce the empirical puzzle, then present the "Pathways to De-dollarization" framework, and finally discuss our research design and data sources.

2.1 An Understudied Issue: De-dollarization through BRICS

A major area of focus for existing *scholarship on international monetary relations, currency power, and economic statecraft* has been the establishment of the US dollar as the world's dominant currency (both as the most commonly held reserve currency and as the most widely used currency for international settlement), and its implications for US global leadership. Scholars have thoroughly investigated the US dollar's currency power from the perspective of the dollar's international currency status.[2] Since the global financial crisis, many scholars have reevaluated the role of the US dollar in the global economy and with respect to US global leadership. They explained how the international use of the US dollar helped build American hegemony; how the dollar's primacy serves as a source of US prestige; and how the United States has used the dollar to assert its global influence (Kirshner, 2008; Goldberg, 2011; Steiner, 2014). Some scholars argued that the root cause of global economic imbalance and the 2007–2008 global financial crisis was the lack of institutionalized currency cooperation (Liu, 2014; Que and Li, 2014). Thus, a proposed postcrisis solution for liquidity surpluses due to ultralow interest rates was to create a multicurrency global reserves system and reduce the dependence on the US dollar (Xiang, 2014).

Historically, the establishment of a dominant currency and the transition from one dominant currency to another did not come as the result of unilateral or collective efforts made by states. For example, the death of the Dutch guilder as a dominant currency in Europe was not the product of the activism of the Bank of England. Rather, the guilder's loss of reserve currency status was primarily due to a permanent market loss of confidence in the Bank of Amsterdam that suffered from policy insolvency, meaning the net worth was negative under its policy objectives (Stella and Lönnberg, 2008; Quinna and Roberds, 2016). Similarly, the Bretton Woods Conference formally recognized the US dollar's global reserve currency status, without the US government imposing this status

---

[2] For example, Kirshner (1995); Blinder (1996), pp. 127–136; Cohen (2002), pp. 5–26; Wheatley (2013).

on other states (Eichengreen and Flandreau, 2008). The Japanese government's attempt to internationalize the yen through multiple mechanisms, such as establishing an offshore market and increasing Japan's foreign aid using the yen, failed due to Japan's economic stagnation since the 1990s (Wu and Wu, 2014). The US dollar's dominance has also been discussed relative to other rising international currencies. Potential challengers to the dollar hegemony are currencies with a growing influence in international monetary affairs. These include the euro, followed by the renminbi.[3] However, the inherent flaws with the euro and renminbi constrain these two currencies' capacity to become the next dominant global currency. In the case of the euro, despite being the second most important global currency after the US dollar, its international role has largely stagnated over the past two decades. The financial market for euro-denominated assets lacks the size and depth of the dollar-denominated market, constraining the euro's capacity to challenge the dollar hegemony in global financial markets. Similarly, the renminbi lags behind the dollar in financial market size and depth. It has the additional problem of a lack of free international capital flows. Thus, scholars have generally agreed that the US dollar remains the world's dominant currency and that no alternative currencies have yet presented a credible challenge to its supremacy (Helleiner and Kirshner, 2009; Eichengreen, 2012). Given the absence of a historical precedent of a rising power de-dollarization coalition, existing research has yet to sufficiently explain the mechanisms and prospects of BRICS' collective de-dollarization initiatives.

Prior research has identified a broad global trend toward financial sector de-dollarization, starting in the early 2000s and continuing until the global financial crisis. However, this trend has generally stalled or even reversed in many countries, with only a few exceptions, such as Peru (Catão et al., 2016). Recent scholarship on economic statecraft has examined de-dollarization activities of countries that are subject to US sanctions and the impact of these activities on US foreign policy and the global monetary system. While acknowledging that countries under US sanctions have a shared incentive to de-dollarize their cross-border settlements, scholars disagree regarding the long-run impact of these individual de-dollarization initiatives on the US dollar's dominance and on the global currency system (Mathew and Selden, 2018; McDowell, 2020; Andermo and Kragh, 2021). Despite the growing theoretical and policy debates on de-dollarization, the extant scholarship has

---

[3] For example, Thygesen et al. (1995); Portes and Rey (1998); Wyplosz (1999); Cohen, Kirshner, and Helleiner (2014); Overholt (2016); Prasad (2016); Subacchi (2016).

not systematically examined coalitional de-dollarization initiatives conducted by a motivated group such as BRICS. Addressing this gap in the existing literature has not only theoretical relevance but also policy implications. An inability to comprehensively understand emerging de-dollarization coalitions could lead US policymakers to neglect and underestimate coalitional challenges to the US global financial leadership.

The contemporary international relations *literature on rising power coalitions* has developed primarily along the dichotomy between rising power alliances and the incumbent power. In this context, rising powers seek to increase their status and influence as agenda-setters and norm-makers in global governance.[4] The alliance concept has traditionally been defined from the hard security perspective as a "formal association of states for the use (or non-use) of military force, in specified circumstances, against states outside their own membership" (Snyder, 1997, p. 4). Recent scholarship has argued that rising powers form versatile alignments rather than security-focused alliances, and that they are unlikely to pursue military alliances to challenge US leadership due to their economic and financial embeddedness in the existing system (Chidley, 2014; Han and Paul, 2020). In the absence of hard balancing and military threats from rising powers, some scholars suggest that rising powers used soft balancing or "nonmilitary tools to delay, frustrate and undermine" US global leadership (Pape, 2005). Such challenges ultimately depend on rising powers' ambitions and whether they are reformers, reform-oriented status quo powers, revolutionaries, counterrevolutionaries, or rational revisionists (Lipton, 2017; Drezner, 2019).

Existing scholarship has theorized about the conditions under which a rising power coalition would pursue various counter-hegemonic strategies. The coalition can challenge the incumbent leadership with a "go-it-alone" (Gruber, 2000) approach: Its members could exclude the United States and operate outside of the existing system, thereby limiting US policy options rather than coercing or persuading the United States to change its ways. Existing global institutions are likely to be challenged in areas where the preferences of the incumbent and the rising powers diverge: these are the areas where states will be motivated to create new institutions (Henning, 2017; Stephen and Parízek, 2019). To exercise collective financial statecraft, a rising power coalition can make reforms within the established system or establish new and competing structures, and it can use institutions and markets as the two venues for action (Katada, Roberts, and Armijo, 2017; Kruck and Zangl, 2020). Although scholars did not specify how

---

[4] For example, Kahler (2013); Schoeman (2015); Mahrenbach (2019).

a rising power coalition can challenge the dollar hegemony, they discussed the core choice of working inside versus outside the system.

Prior scholarship has analyzed rising powers' coalitional counter-hegemonic challenges in the context of their institutional choices, including establishing new institutions and attempting to reform major existing institutions.[5] For example, the China-led Asian Infrastructure Investment Bank (AIIB) is an example of rising powers' counter-hegemonic institutionalism, as it epitomizes the discontent of rising powers with US-led multilateral institutions and the tensions between rising powers and the United States in global economic governance (Ikenberry and Nexon, 2019). However, rising powers' "market choices" and the relevance of the status quo of market instruments for coalitional mobilization have been less discussed. Existing literature has illuminated the potential use of blockchain-based self-executing contracts to achieve trade de-dollarization among small groups of countries, such as BRICS (Aggarwal, 2020). Currency swaps and cryptocurrencies could also be used to de-dollarize global oil trade (Ladasic, 2017). But these proposals have not systematically evaluated the mechanisms through which a collective de-dollarization coalition could be mobilized, and how such a coalition could achieve economies of scale. As a result, existing literature has overlooked the challenge of rising powers' monetary alliances. Thus, it risks underestimating the coalitional scope and credibility of a rising powers alliance, especially if the members of such an alliance have shared frustrations with the dollar and have the financial resources to create their own markets and institutions.

The question of whether BRICS can curb the dollar's "exorbitant privilege" has received attention in the early *literature on BRICS' collective financial statecraft*. Bruetsch and Papa (2013) examined BRICS associational dynamics in the currency realm and found that BRICS generated shared narratives to reduce the dollar's privilege, but its members' divergent interests and disagreements about possible solutions undermined coalitional efforts. Subsequently, scholars have evaluated BRICS' performance both as a financial coalition and as an entity for collective mobilization. Most importantly, BRICS has led emerging markets in changing the global financial order by developing alternative sources of emergency assistance and development financing to create a system that better serves its interests and ideas (Huotari and Hanemann, 2014; Drezner, 2019; Kring and Gallagher, 2019). However, while acknowledging that BRICS financial cooperation is deepening, scholars disagree on the

---

[5] For example, Jupille, Mattli, and Snidal (2013, p25.) defined institutional status quo as "the set of pre-existing institutions potentially relevant to a cooperation problem. These are the institutions available for Use or Selection, or Change."

prospects and credibility of BRICS' initiatives to transform the existing global system. Some have doubts regarding BRICS' potential to act as a system transformer, whereas others hold that the format of BRICS as an informal institution may allow it to gain considerable power (Cooper and Farooq, 2013). Gallagher (2015) reconciled these scholarly differences by providing evidence to demonstrate that it is possible for BRICS to "take advantage of a fragmented and disparate global economic governance landscape to leverage benefits" under unique circumstances.

A prerequisite for BRICS to present itself as a credible de-dollarization coalition is its ability to create a robust coalition. Although existing literature has not explicitly discussed the robustness of BRICS' collective de-dollarization initiatives, it has shown that BRICS has exercised "collective financial statecraft" to challenge the existing liberal international order (Roberts et al., 2017). In particular, institutions such as the NDB and the CRA are examples of BRICS' collective mobilization to reform global financial governance (Chin, 2014; Biziwick, Cattaneo, and Fryer, 2015; Qobo and Soko, 2015; Cooper, 2017; Suchodolski and Demeulemeester, 2018). BRICS has not only transformed the traditional power structures within the existing system, such as the World Trade Organization, but also served as the foundation for broader developing-country coalitions to challenge US hegemony (Hopewell, 2017).

Other scholars are more critical of BRICS' collective mobilization. Some argue that BRICS is unlikely to become a plausible anti-Western alliance that can credibly undermine US leadership and transform the existing international order (e.g., Luckhurst, 2013). BRICS' ability to change the existing system is arguably undermined by the group's political, economic, and ideological heterogeneity (Radulescu, Panait, and Voica, 2014; Tierney, 2014; Li, 2019); the power asymmetry within BRICS (Pandit, 2019); and its lack of a collective world order vision marketable to the broader international community (Nuruzzaman, 2020). Even in development finance, which is often cited as evidence that BRICS is a counter-hegemonic group, scholars contend that the different development assistance models among individual members could weaken a coherent BRICS model (Lauria and Fumagalli, 2019). BRICS' failed attempt at creating its own credit rating agency is a demonstration of the group's limited capacity to transform the global financial order through collective institutional innovation (Helleiner and Wang, 2018).

Finally, among prior scholarship that examined BRICS financial cooperation through the cases of the NDB and the CRA, a few evaluated the outlook of de-dollarization through these BRICS-governed multilateral financial institutions (Chossudovsky, 2018; Kievich, 2018). However, existing research has not fully investigated the wide range of de-dollarization initiatives that BRICS members have experimented with. Nor has it systematically explored the nature of BRICS' "coalitional de-dollarization." This extant research also lacks a comprehensive analysis of how BRICS has engaged with other non-BRICS actors to achieve economies of scale for their de-dollarization initiatives.

2.2 The Puzzle: Is BRICS a De-dollarization Coalition?

It is puzzling why BRICS remains understudied as a de-dollarization coalition for two reasons. First, given the aggregate size of the BRICS economies and markets, as well as the risk of sanctions, the BRICS countries should theoretically have the collective motivation to de-dollarize their international settlements to reduce currency and sanction risks. Historically, all five members have experienced US sanctions, with Russia and China still under various levels of US sanctions. The shared frustrations of the five members should provide strong incentives for them to mobilize toward de-dollarization. Second, reducing dependence on the US dollar and diversifying the global currency and financial system was a publicly declared priority for BRIC when the group first gathered in 2009. When South Africa joined in 2010, BRICS reiterated its shared interest in this issue. Since BRICS is the first rising power coalition with a strong commitment to reforming global financial governance, examining its de-dollarization initiatives presents a unique opportunity for advancing scholarly research on the political economy of coalitional de-dollarization.

The BRICS countries also face a dilemma: While they would prefer to have alternatives to the US dollar as the dominant currency, the dollar's depreciation would decrease the value of their large holdings of dollar-denominated assets. Thus, they need to balance between their desire for greater international influence and financial autonomy and the material costs of weakening the US dollar's dominant currency position. This balancing is not only a critical issue for BRICS, but it also has direct policy implications for other countries and regional organizations. Given BRICS' political and economic significance, its coalitional de-dollarization initiatives will directly impact the US dollar's dominance in the existing global financial system and US global leadership.

While outlining this research puzzle, it is also important to clarify that de-dollarization in this study should not be confused with replacing the US dollar with another global hegemonic currency. BRICS de-dollarization initiatives are not about the group's collective support for renminbi internationalization or the internationalization of any other national currency. This research focuses on *coalitional* de-dollarization pathways and seeks to capture important mechanisms that the five members have pursued to reduce their dependence on the US dollar. Additionally, this research focuses on de-dollarization in the context of international settlements rather than domestic monetary de-dollarization.

2.3 The Analytical Framework: Pathways to De-dollarization

Our analytical framework builds on the assumption that given the tangible costs of being completely isolated from the dollar-based system, members of a rising power coalition do not voluntarily initiate a wholesale revolution against the system. Instead, their de-dollarization initiatives are likely to be reactive to the dollar's dominance, seeking to correct the "destabilizing asymmetry" (Carney, 2019) of the dollar's hegemonic power in the global economic and financial system. Thus, they aim to mitigate the risk of being subject to the US dollar's hegemonic power so as to achieve higher autonomy and seek broader influence in the global system.

A de-dollarization coalition is likely to emerge when members of the dollar-based system are dissatisfied with the international status quo, including the dollar's exorbitant privilege, the incumbent US global leadership, and the existing rules and norms. Rising powers continuously renegotiate the international status quo as they seek to increase their influence and status, aspiring to become rule-makers and agenda-setters in global finance (Cohen, 2005a, 2005b, 2018). However, their dissatisfaction with the system is particularly pronounced and gives rise to a counter-hegemonic coalition when they face direct threats to their financial and geopolitical autonomy. Such threats include being targeted by hostile and coercive policies or having the existing system experience a severe crisis or a shock. The former occurs when, for example, the international financial infrastructure (e.g., SWIFT) is deployed to coerce a targeted actor to change its behavior (Farrell and Newman, 2019; Drezner, Farrell, and Newman, 2021). This leads the actor to turn against the hegemon and build coalitions to resist external pressure. In the latter case, the shared frustration with the crisis and the perceived decline of the existing dollar-based system enabled the rise of coalitional de-dollarization initiatives. Coalitions can help their members survive the crisis and steer the system toward their preferred outcomes. For the de-dollarization coalition to materialize, coalitional members must have the political and economic capacity to influence the dollar system (Goddard, 2018).

Our proposed "Pathways to De-dollarization" framework conceptualizes various channels through which a rising power coalition and its members can mitigate the risk of operating in the dollar-based system. Rising powers can mitigate this risk using two main approaches (drawing on Hirschman, 1970; Gruber, 2000). One approach is to hedge the risk by developing an alternative nondollar-based system that allows rising powers to maintain direct economic and financial connections with other countries in the world without resorting to the dollar-based system. This is the "go-it-alone" strategy, referring to de-dollarization policy options outside the existing dollar-based system and building new, nondollar structures. The other approach is to pursue risk insurance and risk diversification by using "voice" to initiate changes and improve the existing dollar-based system. This is the "reform the status quo" strategy, referring to the pursuit of reforms within the existing system to dilute the dollar's dominant currency status.

These two approaches are not mutually exclusive. First, the "go-it-alone" strategy can create an "exit" from the existing system. However, this strategy cannot be completely separated from the existing system because it still depends on it to mobilize the necessary resources to challenge the system. Second, rising powers may use the potential "exit" as a source of leverage when reforming the existing system, so the threats of exit and parallel institutions serve as a means to increase voice in incumbent institutions (Lipscy, 2015). Finally, in their pursuit of autonomy and influence, rising powers can engage with both *institutional mechanisms* and *market mechanisms* to implement both strategies. Table 1 visualizes the Pathways to De-dollarization framework by offering an illustrative list of common pathways.

Based on this analysis, we propose the following:

Proposition 1: When rising powers seek greater financial and geopolitical autonomy in response to a perceived threat of sanctions and currency risk, they are likely to focus on developing and accelerating "go-it-alone" strategies that emphasize the creation of new nondollar-based institutional and market mechanisms. While developing alternative institutions and markets is a long-term project and requires significant resources, rising powers would pursue fairly low-cost and near-term "reform-the-status quo" strategies to increase access to the existing trading system and global capital by using nondollar currencies and diffusing the dollar's dominance. A rising power coalition can promote the use of local currency in the existing global trading system to weaken the US dollar's dominant vehicle currency status. Its members can reduce their own holdings of US dollar reserves or dollar-denominated assets to defend themselves from currency and sanction-related risks. The coalition can also seek to diversify the existing global currency composition by promoting alternative currencies, such as other national currencies, supranational currencies, or even digital currencies. Finally, coalitional members can also create and expand nondollar-based equity markets in the existing global financial system to divert capital away from the dollar-based markets.

Table 1 Pathways to de-dollarization: Institutional and market mechanisms (an illustrative list)

Risk mitigation mechanisms	Risk mitigation strategy	
	"Go-it-alone"	**"Reform-the-status-quo"**
Institutions	Create new multilateral financial institutions for nondollar financing outside the existing institutions	Strengthen central banks' self-defense against the dollar hegemony and improve emergency access to dollar liquidity
	Promote and popularize nondollar institutions through broader engagement	Reform and diversify existing global reserve currency structure
Markets	Create new alternative nondollar financial instruments and assets in the market	Diffuse the dollar's dominance as the vehicle currency and promote the use of local currency in cross-border transactions
	Create and promote alternative nondollar financial infrastructures for the market	Rearrange global equity market structure and create nondollar equity markets alliance

Applied to the BRICS context, we hypothesize that Russia, as a country continuously under Western sanctions, as well as other economies that are negatively affected by the dollar volatilities, would be leading BRICS' "go-it-alone" de-dollarization strategy, mobilizing other BRICS countries around de-dollarization initiatives and using a wide range of de-dollarization pathways. Threatened rising power coalition members would not only seek to mobilize other BRICS countries around a de-dollarization agenda but are likely to also promote nondollar mechanisms to attract more participants – non-incumbent powers and non-Western organizations such as the Shanghai Cooperation Organization (SCO) to create the economies of scale.

Proposition 2: When rising powers are not under an immediate threat of sanctions, they are likely to stay loyal to the US dollar system and prioritize "reform the status quo" strategies in the near term. The dominant currency paradigm literature suggests that the US dollar's wide use in international transactions pulls other countries into the dollar-based system (Gopinath et al., 2020; Gopinath and Stein, 2021). However, while some path dependence can be assumed in the short term, ambitious rising powers seeking to diversify the system will use both "reform the status quo" and "go-it-alone" de-dollarization strategies to increase their financial and geopolitical influence. Figure 1 visualizes the key areas of US dollar hegemony that a larger de-dollarization mobilization needs to consider.

Figure 1 categorizes the various expressions of the US dollar's dominant currency status into three primary areas: real economy, funding, and invest-ability. These three overarching categories cover the specific areas that constitute the structural constraint that any reactive de-dollarization initia-tive has to consider. More specifically, the US dollar is the dominant global reserve currency and enjoys the highest weight in the Special Drawing Rights (SDR) basket. It is also the dominant invoicing currency in inter-national trade; the leading currency across global financial infrastructure; and, it has the dominant pricing power in major global commodities. The dollar also dominates the space of development financing, bank deposits, and global corporate borrowing. Finally, the dollar is the leading currency in terms of investability as it dominates global equity markets and is the primary safe-haven currency in times of economic and financial crises.

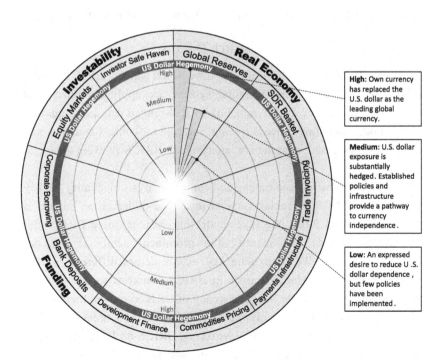

Figure 1 A visualization of the US dollar's dominance

Applied to the BRICS context, since all of the five BRICS countries seek greater financial and geopolitical influence, we hypothesize that they will challenge the dominance of the US dollar by deploying de-dollarization pathways that address these strategic areas, and we measure the level of the challenge on a spectrum from low to high.

Finally, the most comprehensive and effective challenge to the dollar hegemony is if a rising power coalition wages a systematic coalitional de-dollarization campaign and uses a combination of both "go-it-alone" and "reform-the-status-quo" approaches that challenge all the specified areas in which the dollar enjoys dominance. A coalition that can most effectively achieve de-dollarization is one that creates a nondollar club good (e.g., a new institution or market mechanism) that it can govern and use as leverage. Such a coalition can promote the good through broader engagement and even popularize it as a public good to establish an alternative nondollar global system. The "go-it-alone" strategy is more likely than the "reform-the-status -quo" approach to generate such new nondollar club goods. Successful de-dollarization initiatives can not only help rising powers bypass coercive actions but also be weaponized for coercive purposes, and rivals might be denied access. As the initiators of such de-dollarization mechanisms, rising powers would be the dominant rule-makers in a de-dollarized system, likely constraining US policy space and enjoying higher status than their followers.

2.4 Research Design

To examine BRICS' de-dollarization pathways and whether BRICS can de-dollarize the US-led global financial system, we apply the introduced framework and analyze a wide range of BRICS-related data using qualitative methods, including process tracing, interviews, content analysis, and archival research and quantitative analysis of BRICS-relevant financial data.

First, we combine process tracing and content analysis to identify the key milestones in BRICS' financial cooperation and de-dollarization initiatives between 2009 and 2021. We investigate the existence of a BRICS de-dollarization agenda and identify the prominent actors in the de-dollarization space. We triangulate key events across different sources ranging from credible local sources in BRICS countries to international media. Second, to evaluate the consistency of BRICS' commitment to de-dollarization over time, we analyze a variety of archival sources, including speeches and essays by BRICS policymakers, BRICS declarations, BRICS think tank reports, NDB press releases and funding operations, and BRICS

Business Council reports. Third, to get a more accurate picture of BRICS policy preferences, we rely upon semi-structured interviews with experts, officials (current and former), central bankers, and financial professionals in BRICS countries who have either participated in BRICS policymaking or published on the issue of BRICS financial cooperation. We identified experts based on our analysis of BRICS documents, credible news reports, BRICS think tanks' members, and academic publications in leading journals.

We apply the analytical framework by examining a wide range of BRICS de-dollarization initiatives comprising the use of both institutional and market mechanisms to mitigate BRICS members' risk exposure to the dollar's hegemonic power. These initiatives include the NDB and development finance de-dollarization; global oil trade de-dollarization; global financial infrastructure de-dollarization through BRICS alternatives to SWIFT; BRICS promotion of de-dollarization initiatives by engaging with non-BRICS members; self-defense measures in US-led institutions against the dollar's dominance; reforms of the global reserve currency structure; efforts to diffuse the dollar's dominance as the vehicle currency in trade; and BRICS' activities in global equity markets. Our Pathways framework allows us to identify and evaluate what members have achieved, and the benchmark of strategic de-dollarization areas illustrates what BRICS should do to de-dollarize. The combination of the two approaches allows us to zoom in and examine the specific strategies each BRICS member pursues, as well as distinguish the BRICS countries leading de-dollarization efforts from the less active members. The resulting analysis allows us to evaluate the overall level of the BRICS' de-dollarization challenge.

To understand the extent of collective mobilization along the pathways proposed in our framework, we introduce a two-dimensional matrix measuring the effectiveness of de-dollarization initiatives and the level of coalitional strength. The benchmark for a high level of effectiveness is the creation of nondollar institutions and/or market instruments or market infrastructure. Following our conceptualization, the "go-it-alone" strategy leads to a higher level of de-dollarization effectiveness, as it targets the creation of new nondollar mechanisms. In contrast, the "reform-status-quo" strategy yields lower effectiveness due to its lack of mechanism innovations. We measure coalitional strength by the number of participants in a de-dollarization initiative. This is because cross-border settlements in international trade and finance require counterparties and the formation of a nondollar global financial system requires broad participation of state actors and non-state actors. A higher number of participants means that a de-dollarization initiative is more robust. Unilateral initiatives may be potentially scaled to the coalitional level, but they represent a low level of coalitional strength. The coalitional strength increases as more members of the rising power coalition jointly participate in de-dollarization initiatives. Once the coalition builds full consensus, it demonstrates greater coalitional strength. When the rising power coalition expands its de-dollarization initiatives beyond the group members and mobilizes a broader coalition, the coalitional strength is the highest. As Figure 1 illustrates, the combination of high effectiveness and high coalitional strength is in the upper right cell, which features the formation of an alternative nondollar global financial system that is governed by rising powers and not the United States (Figure 2).

We augment our qualitative analysis with quantitative data from the NDB's annual reports, its project database, SWIFT reports and statistics, Bank for International Settlements international locational banking statistics, treasuries holdings data from Bloomberg, the Treasury International Capital System, commodities futures data from the Shanghai Futures Exchange, BRICS reserves data and trading data from the People's Bank of China, Bank of Russia, South African Reserve Bank, Reserve Bank of India, Central Bank of Brazil, ICE Benchmark Administration, and World Gold Council, and BRICS voting rights data and SDR quota from the World Bank and the IMF.

3 BRICS as a De-dollarization Coalition

This section investigates whether BRICS can be considered a de-dollarization coalition. Combining process tracing with content analysis, it first analyzes how BRICS as a financial coalition has addressed the issue of diversifying the US dollar-based global financial and currency system since the group's establishment in 2009. Next, this section assesses the state of BRICS currencies in global currency markets in order to examine the dynamics of BRICS currencies relative to the dollar's dominant position. Finally, it investigates individual BRICS countries' perspectives on de-dollarization to evaluate the convergence of their interests; who is advocating for de-dollarization and how; and how mobilization around de-dollarization takes place.

3.1 Key Milestones in the Evolution of BRICS as a Financial Coalition

The first BRIC summit in 2009 concluded with a clear statement from its leaders: "[w]e are committed to advancing the reform of international

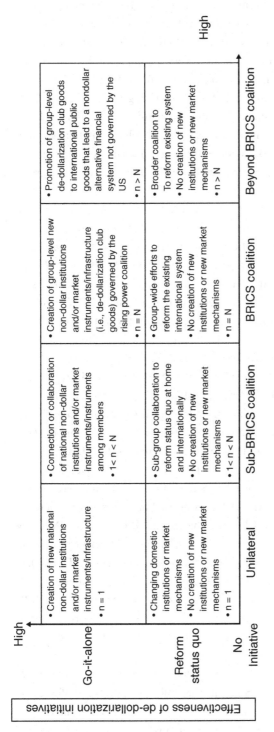

Figure 2 Measuring coalitional de-dollarization initiatives

Note: n = number of participants in a de-dollarization initiative (state and non-state actors N = number of formal members in the rising power coalition (in the case of BRICS, $N = 5$, including Brazil, Russia, India, China, and South Africa).

financial institutions, so as to reflect changes in the global economy ... We also believe that there is a strong need for a stable, predictable and more diversified international monetary system" (BRIC, 2009). Financial cooperation has been a consistent theme during every annual BRICS summit ever since and has been covered in joint summit declarations. Several key milestones energized BRICS' commitment to diversifying the existing system. For example, between 2012 and 2017, BRICS established the NDB, collectively pushed for the use of local currency in development finance, and launched the CRA. In 2020, BRICS identified empowering local currencies as its long-term agenda item, thereby cementing its importance for the group in the future.

The first milestone is the establishment of the NDB and the CRA, which was initially proposed in 2012 and 2013 respectively, though both materialized in 2014. These two institutions resulted from the BRICS members' frustration with their limited progress in reforming the Bretton Woods institutions. BRICS created the NDB and CRA to mirror the functions of the World Bank and the IMF respectively, but operate under BRICS ownership and control. The NDB and CRA were both designed to help BRICS reduce their dependence on US dollar financing and the IMF. For example, in the *Agreement on the New Development Bank*, BRICS states that the NDB "may provide financing in the local currency of the country in which the operation takes place" (NDB, 2014). This statement positioned the NDB as a development finance intermediary that uses local currencies to mobilize capital in international markets and provides financing for its members (see Section 4). This local currency financing function makes the NDB resemble the BRICS own "mini–World Bank." However, the NDB yields greater benefits than the World Bank for BRICS members: NDB loans have fewer strings attached, and local currency loans allow borrowers not to increase external US dollar debt. The CRA was hailed as "BRICS' own IMF" by President Putin because it "creates the foundation for an effective protection of (our) national economies from a crisis in financial markets" (*RT*, 2014). It makes pooled dollar reserves of USD100 billion available to provide liquidity support for members in times of a modest-sized balance of payment (BoP) crisis (BRICS, 2013). Yet, the CRA is not a lender of last resort; rather, it provides the members with the first line of defense before they have to seek conditional help from the IMF (see Section 5).

The most recent de-dollarization milestone was achieved amid the COVID-19 pandemic at the BRICS 2020 Summit when BRICS agreed to reinforce and advance the current de-dollarization processes. Under Russia's chairmanship in 2020, the group jointly issued the *Strategy for BRICS Economic Partnership*

2025. This Strategy reiterated the members' long-standing commitment to reforming the Bretton Woods institutions. More importantly, it identified several "priority areas of partnership" directly related to de-dollarization, including: to promote the use of local currencies in mutual payments, to strengthen BRICS cooperation on payments systems, to collaborate on the development of new financial technologies, to advance the CRA mechanism, to continue cooperation on establishing the BRICS Local Currency Bond Fund, and to continue to facilitate the NDB in development financing while expanding the use of local currencies (BRICS, 2020).

Over the past two decades, BRICS has shown consistent commitment to reforming the global financial system and diversifying the global currency structure. Catalyzed by the global financial crisis and the COVID-19 pandemic, the group has implemented targeted policies and broadened areas of cooperation to help members reduce their dependence on the US dollar. The recent military conflict between India and China did not prevent the coalition members from deepening their economic partnership. This suggests that there is a political will to pursue the economic agenda, and that de-dollarization will remain an important issue for BRICS despite their divergence in other areas.

3.2 The Gradual Rise of BRICS Currencies

As BRICS incrementally implemented specific policies for de-dollarization, BRICS national currencies have progressively gained more market share in the dollar-based global currency system, albeit remaining at relatively low levels compared to the US dollar. The most direct way for BRICS to reduce their dependence on the US dollar is to increase the use of their own national currencies in cross-border transactions. According to the latest Bank for International Settlements Triennial Survey (2019), the Chinese renminbi was the 8th most actively traded currency, ranking just after the Swiss franc. This is a significant increase from its ranking of 35th in 2001. Additionally, the renminbi is now the most actively traded emerging market currency. It reached 4.3 percent of total global turnover in 2019, a significant rise compared with 0.1 percent in 2004. The Indian rupee was the second most traded BRICS currency, in 16th position worldwide and accounting for 1.7 percent of global trade. The Russian ruble, Brazilian real, and South African rand were in 17th, 20th and 33rd position, respectively (Table 2).

Comparing the currency ranking position changes from 2004 to 2019, the increase in the renminbi's active trading turnover was the largest. The growth in trading turnover for other BRICS currencies was not as rapid but nonetheless

Table 2 Over-the-counter foreign exchange turnover by currencies (net-net basis, percentage shares of average daily turnover)

	Currency	2004		2007		2010		2013		2016		2019	
		Share	Rank	Share	Rank	Share	Rank	Share	Rank	Share	Rank	Share	Rank
Leading global	USD	88.0	1	85.6	1	84.9	1	87.0	1	87.6	1	88.3	1
currencies	EUR	37.4	2	37.0	2	39.0	2	33.4	2	31.4	2	32.3	2
	JPY	20.8	3	17.2	3	19.0	3	23.0	3	21.6	3	16.8	3
	GBP	16.5	4	14.9	4	12.9	4	11.8	4	12.8	4	12.8	4
BRICS	CNY[1]	0.1	29	0.5	20	0.9	17	2.2	9	4.0	8	4.3	8
currencies	INR[1]	0.3	20	0.7	19	0.9	15	1.0	20	1.1	18	1.7	16
	RUB[1]	0.6	17	0.7	18	0.9	16	1.6	12	1.1	17	1.1	17
	BRL[1]	0.3	21	0.4	21	0.7	21	1.1	19	1.0	19	1.1	20
	SAR[2]	0.0	33	0.1	33	0.1	33	0.1	34	0.3	26	0.2	33
Other currencies		36	-	42.9	-	40.7	-	38.8	-	39.1	-	41.4	-
Total[3]		200	-	200	-	200	-	200	-	200	-	200	-

1. Turnover for years prior to 2013 may be underestimated owing to incomplete reporting of offshore trading in previous surveys. Methodological changes in the 2013 survey ensured more complete coverage of activity in EME and other currencies.

2. Turnover may be underestimated owing to incomplete reporting of offshore trading.

3. Because two currencies are involved in each transaction, the sum of the percentage shares of individual currencies totals 200 percent instead of 100 percent.

Sources: Author compiled data from Bank for International Settlements (BIS) "Triennial Central Bank Survey of Foreign Exchange and Over-the-Counter (OTC) Derivatives Markets," December 2019.

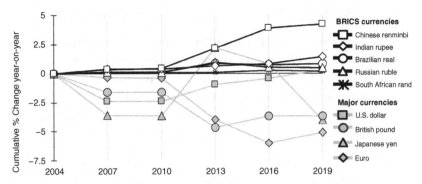

Figure 3 Currency distribution of over-the-counter (OTC) foreign exchange turnover

Source: Author compiled data from Bank for International Settlements (BIS) "Triennial Central Bank Survey of Foreign Exchange and Over-the-Counter (OTC) Derivatives Markets," December 2019.

steady. In contrast, the shares of leading global currencies, especially the euro, Japanese yen, and the British pound sterling have generally decreased, although they were still three of the top four most actively traded currencies. Trading in US dollars decreased for the two surveys in 2007 and 2010, largely due to the global financial crisis and the US dollar liquidity crunch, but it quickly recovered in the following years (Table 2 and Figure 3).

This currency trading activity comparison reveals that the US dollar still maintains its absolute dominance in the currency market. However, the collective market share of BRICS currencies, especially renminbi, has slowly increased, but it is still far smaller than the US dollar's market share. However, the small increase in the market share of BRICS currencies did not cause the US dollar's market share to decrease, as the US dollar's share has remained stable. As the BRICS countries implement their currency internationalization policies, trading activities of BRICS currencies will slowly increase. This increase may not necessarily come at the expense of the US dollar; rather, it may erode the market share of other major currencies, as data from 2004 to 2019 demonstrates.

BRICS currencies' slight gain in the OTC foreign exchange market cannot credibly challenge the dollar's dominance in international settlements in any meaningful way. BRICS' insignificant currency share in global markets at present is disproportionate to their combined weight of approximately 16 percent of global trade (BRICS India, 2021). This discrepancy illustrates both the dollar's dominance and the difficulty of achieving de-dollarization.

3.3 BRICS Members' Perspectives on De-dollarization

Recognizing the heterogeneity within BRICS, the analysis now turns to investigating whether BRICS members have demonstrated a shared interest in de-dollarization by examining their respective official discourses.

China's advocacy for reforming the dollar-based global financial system can be traced back to the 1997 Asian financial crisis. In the aftermath of this crisis, Dai Xianglong, then Governor of the People's Bank of China (PBoC), stated:

> "The current international monetary and financial system can no longer accommodate the needs of international economic and financial development, and, therefore, the system needs to be reformed . . .. The role of international reserve currency played by a few countries' national currency has been a major source of instability in the international monetary system . . . The current international financial system cannot solve the balance of payments imbalance, which has repeatedly been the cause of international financial crises" (Dai,1999).

Following the 2007–2008 global financial crisis, Dai's successor Zhou Xiaochuan (Zhou 2009) openly discussed the necessity of reforming the international monetary system and called for the creation of "an international reserve currency that is disconnected from individual nations" because the prevailing system's deficiencies were "caused by using credit-based national currencies." Zhou's view is believed to represent the thoughts of leading Chinese officials who see the era of a US dollar-dominated world is coming to an end.[6] In 2011, President Hu Jintao commented that "[t]he current international currency system is the product of the past" (*Washington Post*, 2011).

Although there is no indication that high-level Chinese policymakers explicitly discussed dethroning the US dollar as the leading reserve currency, we find that Chinese academics and observers have frequently criticized dollar hegemony and proposed various means to challenge it. Such proposals have recently proliferated due to the deterioration of US - China relations, and growing threats of US sanctions against China in strategic areas such as advanced technology. Strategic rivalry with the United States provides incentives for China to self-insure against risks in the US-led global system, not just for economic reasons but also for geopolitical and strategic reasons. Compared with other BRICS members, China has more resources and is better positioned to promote de-dollarization across several platforms, including but not limited to BRICS. For example, China has been adjusting its strategies for renminbi internationalization through the development of offshore renminbi markets and through bilateral currency swaps in the context of the Belt and

---

[6] Interview with a former Chinese central bank official, February 12, 2021.

Road Initiative. Chinese state-owned commercial banks are also more potent and more globalized compared to banking institutions in other BRICS members. China's policy banks, especially the China Development Bank and Exim Bank of China, now provide as much development financing as the World Bank does (Ray and Simmons, 2020).

Russia has been actively promoting the idea of de-dollarization through BRICS, and its primary motivation for doing so is its geopolitical rivalry with the United States. In 2012, Sergei Ryabkov, Russian Deputy Foreign Minister at the time, publicly expressed Russia's concerns over the US dollar's role as the settlement unit of international trade and banking transactions and affirmed that "it is necessary to become less dependent on the dollar" (Labetskaya, 2012). President Putin (2017) expressed in an article that the BRICS members "are ready to work together with our partners to promote international financial regulation reforms and to overcome the excessive domination of the limited number of reserve currencies." Soon after his article was published, Ryabkov disclosed that it is a "vital need" for Russia to "intensify work related to import substitution, reduction of dependence on US payment systems, on the dollar as a settling currency" (Nikolskaya, 2017).

President Putin began his fourth presidential term in May 2018 with a strong commitment to further de-dollarize the Russian economy and defend Russia's economic sovereignty against US sanctions. In his speech at the Russian parliament Putin called for "getting free of the dollar burden" in the global oil trade and in the Russian economy because the monopoly of the US dollar was "unreliable" and "dangerous" for global trade and the economies of many countries in the world (*TASS*, 2018). In August 2018, discussions on the need to de-dollarize the Russian economy intensified in the Russian government after the US Congress introduced a new bill that targeted Russian financial institutions. In October 2018, the Putin administration backed a tentative de-dollarization plan designed to limit Russia's exposure to future US sanctions by reducing the use of the US dollar in international settlements and conducting international business using alternative currencies (*Invesforesight*, 2018; *RT International*, 2018).

Brazil initially shared Russia's enthusiasm for making BRICS a de-dollarization coalition. Former Brazilian President Lula da Silva argued that "BRICS was not created to be an instrument of defense, but to be an instrument of attack. So we could create our own currency to become independent from the US dollar in our trade relations ... The United States was very much afraid when I discussed a new currency and Obama called me, telling me, 'Are you trying to create a new currency, a new euro?' I said, 'No, I'm just trying to get rid of the US dollar. I'm just trying not to be dependent'" (Escobar, 2019). It is not irrational for President Lula to have proposed de-dollarizing Brazil's trade. The US dollar dominated Brazil's exports invoicing, as high as 94 percent, although exports to the United States were only 17 percent of Brazil's total exports (Casas et al., 2017). Our interviews suggest that there are three primary reasons that incentivized Brazil to follow Russia and China's de-dollarization initiatives but not take the lead. First, Brazil's severe economic crisis since 2014 following the end of the commodity boom has fragmented the country's politics and led to the rise of the right-wing Bolsonaro administration. Under President Bolsonaro, the Brazilian government has sent mixed signals regarding its BRICS policy and has moved closer to Western powers. Second, Brazil has become more reliant on commodities exports, making the country more exposed to volatilities in global markets and currency risks (see also Nogueira Batista Jr., 2019). According to UNCTADstat, Brazil's commodity exports represented 56.5 percent of total exports in 2008–2009. This number has increased to 66.6 percent over the past ten years. Third, China has been Brazil's most important trading partner, and the economic and financial ties between the two countries have increasingly become closer. The use of local currencies in bilateral settlements is beneficial for both sides. Brazil's close economic and financial ties with China and the real risks to the Brazilian economy due to its dependence on the US dollar suggest that Brazil is unlikely to openly champion BRICS de-dollarization initiatives. However, it is open to playing along and following them.

India was reluctant to join a BRICS de-dollarization coalition from the very beginning despite its support for other key issues on the BRICS agenda, such as reforming the IMF and World Bank (*Economic Times*, 2009). When Russia and China proposed to create a new global super-sovereign reserve currency to replace the US dollar in 2009 (Shchedrov, 2009; Zhou, 2009), India distanced itself from such a challenge to the US dollar's supremacy but instead preferred a more modest approach of increasing the IMF's SDR. The Indian government considered this Sino-Russian proposal more ideological than substantive and did not want to challenge the US dollar and upset the United States, especially at a time when the United States was pressuring Pakistan on counterterrorism (*Economic Times*, 2009). While the United States treats Russia and China as strategic competitors, it considers India as an important ally in the Indo-Pacific region and an important strategic partner. India's rivalry with China and the recent military standoff between the two countries have further prevented India from supporting China's attempt to replace the US dollar.[7] In the context of

---

[7] Interview with an Indian expert, June 18, 2021.

BRICS, this means India will not support an explicit BRICS mobilization to dethrone the US dollar.

This by no means suggests that India is satisfied with the US dollar's dominance and would not seek to reduce its dependence on the US dollar. On the contrary, India not only has a strong interest in promoting the use of local currency in trade but also has taken initiatives to explore how to accomplish this. In 2012, India's Ministry of Commerce and Industry convened a Task Force to examine the use of the rupee in India's bilateral trade. The Task Force Report favored the idea of extending rupee trade to some oil-exporting countries (Dash, Sharma, and Nizami, 2019). The Indian government formed a multi-agency task force with representatives from India's economic policymaking agencies to draw up a list of countries with which India could trade in rupees.[8] India has also taken the lead in promoting BRICS financial cooperation and building BRICS financial institutions. For example, it was at the behest of the Indian finance minister that the BRICS in 2012 commissioned a joint working group to study the viability of setting up a BRICS Development Bank, which led to the creation of the NDB that promotes the use of local currencies in development finance. India has also promoted greater use of the rupee in international transactions in light of aggressive steps by China to internationalize the renminbi and US sanctions on Russia and Iran in 2018, which disrupted India's oil payments in US dollars. The increase in currency exchange volatilities – especially growing volatilities in the US dollar – provides another incentive for India to de-dollarize its trade settlement, as India is among the most dollarized countries in trade invoicing (Gajara, 2020). To give some context, 86 percent of India's imports relied on US dollar invoicing despite only 5 percent of India's imports originating in the United States. Similarly, 86 percent of India's exports were invoiced in US dollars, while only 15 percent of India's exports were to the United States (Casas, et al., 2017; Gopinath and Zwaanstra. 2017). Therefore, although India is unlikely to play an explicit role in a BRICS coalition aiming to dethrone the US dollar, it will implicitly help reduce dollar dependence by supporting initiatives that promote the use of local currencies in trade and development finance.

South Africa saw US sanctions imposed against it in 1986 mostly lifted by 1991, and with the dismantling of apartheid, the relationship between the two countries has improved (Friedman, 1991). The strength of this relationship partly explains South Africa's lack of a strong de-dollarization agenda. In the

---

[8] The task force was formed with representatives from the Commerce Ministry, the Department of Economic Affairs, the Reserve Bank of India, State Bank of India, the Federation of Indian Chambers of Commerce and Industry, the Confederation of Indian Industry, and the Federation of Indian Exporters Organization. See Amiti and Mishra (2014).

course of our research, we did not find any public records of South African leaders promoting the idea of BRICS as a de-dollarization coalition. Yet, South Africa follows Russia and China's de-dollarization efforts. Our interviews with scholars in South Africa reveal that South African policymakers are keenly aware of the risks associated with the US dollar's privilege.[9] Both the real economic risk and transaction risk due to the US dollar's dominance incentivize South Africa to go along with BRICS' initiatives to promote the use of local currencies in trade. South African leaders have publicly expressed South Africa's interests in this issue. Following the 2011 BRICS Summit, South African Trade and Industry Minister Rob Davies said that BRICS members could protect themselves from exchange volatilities and benefit considerably by trading directly in their own currencies and cutting out unstable internationally convertible currencies – specifically, the US dollar (*Brand South Africa*, 2011). During the 2013 BRICS Summit, Davies reiterated South Africa's interest in working out a mechanism within BRICS to settle trade in local currencies and emphasized that currency market volatility in developing countries "takes place not really because of any dynamics in our own country but because of dynamics in the world economy" (*Economic Times*, 2013). This reflects the challenging macroeconomic conditions that developing countries face in global markets as price takers whose currency risk can be triggered by factors beyond their control. Davies' comments expressed not only South Africa's frustration over its lack of autonomy in achieving economic security in global markets but also a shared frustration among developing countries within and beyond the BRICS group. There has not been any formal reporting about a unilateral South African push for de-dollarization, but the country has supported BRICS' general agreement on promoting the use of local currencies in international trade and finance. South Africa has also accepted broader use of the Chinese renminbi and has included renminbi in its foreign exchange reserves to diversify currency risk. SWIFT data shows that between 2013 and 2015, the number of South Africa's renminbi payments increased by 191 percent, and by June 2015, the value of direct payments in renminbi between South Africa and China/Hong Kong reached 31.3 percent (SWIFT, 2015).

To summarize, BRICS has demonstrated a consistent commitment to reforming the US dollar-based global financial system, as evidenced by the group's deepening cooperation on de-dollarization. Although not all BRICS members want to explicitly challenge the US dollar, there is a shared interest in reducing their dependence on it. All BRICS members have taken concrete

---

[9] Interview with a former official at South Africa's National Treasury, January 7, 2021; interview with two South African think tank researchers working on BRICS economic and finance issues, January 12 and 20, 2021; interview with a senior economist at South African Reserve Bank (SARB), February 3, 2021.

steps towards de-dollarization with the aim of achieving greater autonomy. BRICS has also implemented targeted policies to help members reduce their dependence on the US dollar through the promotion of local currencies in trade and investment, both at the BRICS level and the sub-BRICS level.

Our analysis shows that there have been clear leaders within BRICS attempting to steer the group toward a de-dollarization coalition, namely Russia and to a lesser extent China. Their primary motivation for de-dollarization includes rising geopolitical rivalries with the United States and the growing risk of US sanctions. Our analysis reveals that Russia and China have taken different approaches to de-dollarization. In line with our first proposition, Russia has been far more aggressive in its attempts to protect its economy from US sanctions and has been the most enthusiastic advocate of de-dollarization within BRICS. Russian policymakers are vocal about the topic in public, laying out the case for de-dollarization and its importance. In contrast, China has made less noise but has been more capable of making substantive changes. China has not openly talked about de-dollarization, but it has emphasized its desire to "diversify" the system. The diversification of the system is a positive framing that focuses on China's prioritization of the system's stability and equality rather than the potentially counter-hegemonic nature of such actions. BRICS is one of several platforms it can use to pursue de-dollarization.

Our analysis also shows that the followers in BRICS de-dollarization coalition are neither passive nor silent. Brazil, India, and South Africa have all supported BRICS joint statements on reforming the existing dollar-centered global financial system over the past two decades. Moreover, they each have also sought opportunities to promote the use of local currencies in international trade and development financing. Their consensus and practices concerning de-dollarization suggest that de-dollarization does not only take place in countries that are in geopolitical competition with the United States or under US sanctions. Rather, de-dollarization is important for developing countries that are price takers in global markets and lack autonomy in controlling their own economic security. Therefore, it is a real priority for these countries to diversify and reduce their risk exposure to exogenous shocks and exchange volatilities due to the US dollar's dominance. This creates a baseline of shared interests among all countries that are subject to the US dollar's privilege, whether they are US allies or adversaries.

4 "Go-It-Alone" Strategy: Establishing New Institutions and Market Mechanisms

This section examines BRICS' "go-it-alone" strategy through both institution-building and market-building that create critical components for an alternative nondollar global financial system. As a rising power coalition, BRICS has created a group-level de-dollarization club good with a relatively high level of effectiveness by establishing and using the NDB to de-dollarize development finance. BRICS has also shown a commitment to developing other new de-dollarization club goods such as a common BRICS payment system to facilitate settlement using local currencies and a BRICS digital currency. At the sub-BRICS level, members have launched nondollar national payment systems that could form the basis for a BRICS alternative to the US dollar-dominated SWIFT. They have also been exploring options for central bank digital currencies, and China has already launched its digital renminbi. China has successfully launched a new nondollar market instrument, yuan oil futures, to de-dollarize global oil trade. Collectively, BRICS members have leveraged their overlapping membership in non-Western multilateral organizations (e.g., the SCO) to promote the use of local currencies in international trade and finance and create new outreach opportunities for broader de-dollarization.

4.1 The New Development Bank and De-dollarizing Development Finance

The NDB has already raised funds in local currencies as part of its goal to "break away from the tyranny of hard currencies," as the NDB President Mr. Kamath put it (*RT International*, 2017). It has implemented a local currency lending program that not only helps member countries mitigate the borrowers' foreign exchange risk but also supports the development of local capital markets. The NDB also prioritizes the "use of borrowing country legislation, regulations and oversight procedures" whenever possible, as it sees "using national system as the best way to strengthen a country's own capacity and achieve better long-term development results" (NDB, 2017, pp. 15–16). Through these programs, the NDB helps the BRICS countries improve their financial autonomy by reducing their reliance on dollar financing.

The establishment of the NDB first and foremost allows for the BRICS countries to borrow from international capital markets at a much lower rate because the NDB has been able to obtain a higher credit rating than most of the BRICS members. Since the NDB was established in 2014, Brazil, Russia, and South Africa have experienced several rounds of credit downgrading into 'junk' territory.[10] Their deteriorated credit ratings then increased their borrowing costs

---

[10] In September 2015, Brazil was downgraded by S&P to BB+, highest speculative rating, which was then cut deeper into the junk territory to BB in February 2016, further down to BB- in January 2018. Russia's credit rating was stable at around BBB as rated by S&P from 2008 to early 2014, but was downgraded in April 2014 BBB-, the lowest investment grade, then slid into the junk territory BB+ in September 2016, but regained BBB- rating in February 2018. South

in international capital markets. Although India did not experience a downgrade during this period, its lowest investment-grade rating was not ideal either. Therefore, all five members were committed to obtaining a higher credit rating for the NDB, and they succeeded: the NDB received a credit rating of AA+ from S&P and Fitch, which is higher than any individual BRICS member, China included. This rating allows several BRICS members to borrow from global capital markets at much cheaper rates through the higher-rated NDB than they could on their own. The NDB's high credit rating allows it to raise capital relatively cheaply from the bond markets and lend onward at interest rates lower than what could be obtained by some BRICS sovereign borrowers themselves. The NDB's Vice President Leslie Maasdorp (2019) highlighted the NBD's ability to borrow at a lower cost as "a significant advantage," as it enables the NDB to pass on that benefit in the form of competitive interest rates when it extends loans to its members.

The NDB also helps the BRICS members reduce their reliance on dollar financing by extending loans in local currency and prioritizing local regulations and procedures where appropriate. Mr. Kamath (2020) reported that a quarter of the NDB's cumulative total approved financial assistance (about USD15 billion) was given in local currencies by the end of 2019. Although Kamath said that BRICS had no intention of destabilizing the US dollar, he proposed that "50 percent (of projects) should be local currency financed". He acknowledged that the NDB would raise both dollars and euros, but "at the same time there will be a significant reliance on local currencies," which would "allow the bank to move away from loans denominated in dollars" (Hancock, 2019). The NDB's *General Strategy 2017–2021* considered local currency financing as "a key component of NDB's value proposition, as it mitigates risks faced by borrowers and supports the deepening of capital markets of member countries" (NDB, 2017, p. 4). It will "rely on local currency lending to the extent feasible to avoid foreign exchange risks for borrowers" and will actively seek opportunities to offer local currency loans "both to reduce risks to borrowers as well as to promote local capital markets" (NDB, 2017, pp. 6, 14). Besides promoting local currency lending, the NDB has also approved loans in other currencies such as the euro and the Swiss franc in 2019 to diversify its source of funding away from the US dollar (NDB, 2019, p. 4).

Africa also experienced cascading downgrade since 2014. It was first downgraded from BBB to BBB- in June 2014, then was moved to junk territory to BB+ in April 2017, BB in 2019, and deep down in the junk to BB- in April 2020. India's credit rating was relatively stable around BBB- during this period. For more information, see Leahy (2015); Pacheco (2016); Reuters (2018); "Russia – Credit Rating" (n.d.); "South Africa – Credit Rating" (n.d.).

To reduce the burden of dollar-denominated loans, the NDB must tap into nondollar capital markets for alternative sources of financing. It is also crucial for the NDB to obtain a high-quality credit rating in nondollar markets to reduce its cost of funding. The NDB has been moving in the right direction. It has obtained an AAA rating in capital markets not only within BRICS such as China and Russia but also beyond BRICS such as in Japan.[11] Additionally, Fitch assigned the NDB's "Euro Medium-Term Notes Program" an AA+ rating (Fitch Ratings, 2019). Obtaining a wider credit rating in different currency areas paves the way for the NDB to tap into capital markets in these different currency areas, allowing for the diversification of its funding source. Leslie Maasdorp confirmed this point, arguing that the NDB's "intention is to not only build a dollar curve but also widen out our funding to other currencies, such as sterling and euros" (Khadbai, 2020).

The NDB's AAA credit rating in China allowed it to quickly tap into the Chinese capital market and issue a renminbi bond. Since then, the NDB has become the most active official sector issuer of Panda bonds, renminbi-denominated bonds sold in China by foreign issuers. The NDB had issued six Panda bonds worth RMB18 billion as of March 2021 (Table 3), with the most recent Panda bond issuance taking place in March 2021 when it sold RMB5 billion (USD767 million) Panda bond. This was the NDB's first issuance of the Sustainable Development Goals bond. The bond proceeds were to be used to finance China's RMB7 billion Emergency Program Loan to help mitigate the impact of COVID-19 on the Chinese economy (NDB, 2021).

The NDB also planned to raise local capital funding from other BRICS members' capital markets and has registered bond programs therein. It registered its debut bond program in South Africa in April 2019. The registered maximum size of the bond program was 10 billion rand and is governed by South African law. In November 2019, the NDB also registered its debut ruble bond program in Russia with a maximum size of RUB100 billion. The program was listed on the Moscow Exchange and is covered by the laws of the Russian Federation (NDB, 2019). Additionally, the NDB planned to tap into the Indian

---

[11] The NDB was rated as AAA by two Chinese credit rating agencies (China Chengxin International Credit Rating and China Lianhe Credit Rating) in 2016, AAA with stable outlook by a Russian credit rating agency ACRA, and AAA long-term issuer rating with a stable outlook by Japan Credit Rating Agency, Ltd (JCR). For the original credit rating report by Lianhe Credit Rating, see Lianhe Credit Rating (2016), a 2020 Annual follow-up rating report by China Chengxin International Credit Rating (2020). ACRA affirms AAA to New Development Bank, outlook Stable, under the international scale and AAA(RU), outlook Stable, under the national scale for the Russian Federation, see ACRA Ratings (2020). NDB Obtains AAA Rating from Japan Credit Rating Agency. For the full credit rating report by JCR, see Japan Credit Rating Agency (2019, 2020).

Table 3 NDB renminbi-denominated Bond Issuance (January 2016–March 2021)

Pricing Date	Size	Tenor	Coupon
07/18/2016	RMB3 billion	5 years	3.07%
02/25/2019	RMB2 billion	3 years	3%
	RMB1 billion	5 years	3.32%
04/02/2020	RMB5 billion	3 years	2.43%
07/07/2020	RMB 2 billion	5 years	3%
03/24/2021	RMB 5 billion	3 years	3.22%

Source: Author compiled data from NDB website, Bloomberg Financial, and Global Capital China Panda Bond database.

rupee-denominated masala (foreign-issued) bond market in the second half of 2017, but this was postponed due to a significant drop in market liquidity and demand for masala bonds. However, the NDB has remained interested in the Indian rupee offshore market as part of its capital raising (*Hindu Business Line*, 2019).

Finally, the NDB helps its members with local currency loans. By the end of 2019, cumulative approved local currency loans represented 27 percent of the NDB's total portfolio (Figure 4 and Table 4). This number is remarkable because it is higher than the local currency loan percentages of other major multilateral development banks. This higher percentage is likely due to the fact that the NDB has been offering renminbi loans since the beginning of its operations. The NDB also approved its first rand-denominated loans amounting to USD1.2 billion equivalent in 2019. By the end of 2019, about two-thirds of the NDB's cumulative approvals for projects located in China were denominated in renminbi, and about half of its lending to South African borrowers was made in rand. This shows that the NDB has made good on its pledge to extend loans in local currencies.

4.2 The Yuan Oil Futures and De-dollarizing Global Oil Trade

While the NDB represents a BRICS' coalitional challenge to the US dollar's dominance by establishing a new multilateral institution governed by its members, there are also important de-dollarization trends in the global oil market that can be augmented by expanding BRICS energy cooperation.[12] The US dollar's

---

[12] BRICS members hold regular meetings among their energy ministers. The group has established the BRICS Energy Research Cooperation Platform and has also developed a Roadmap for BRICS Energy Cooperation 2025 (BRICS-Russia, 2020).

Table 4 NDB cumulative loan approvals by currency (2018–2019)

Currency	As of December 31, 2019		As of December 31, 2018	
	Number	$ Equivalent	Number	$ Equivalent
RMB	9	2,768	5	1,558
ZAR	4	1,235	—	—
CHF	1	516	—	—
EUR	1	500	—	—
USD	36	9,914	25	6,270
Total	51	14,933	30	7,828

Source: Author compiled data from NDB annual report (2019).

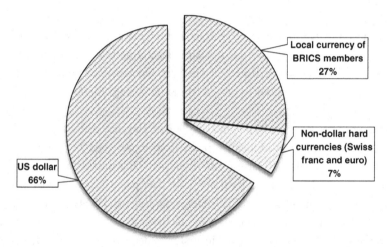

Figure 4 NDB Cumulative loan approvals by type of currency (as of December 31, 2019)

Source: Author compiled data from NDB official website and NDB annual report (2019, 2020).

hegemonic position in the global financial system has been critically grounded in its exclusive position as the funding vehicle and pricing currency of the global oil trade. The world's leading crude oil pricing benchmarks, namely the West Texas Intermediate (WTI) and Brent, are priced in US dollars. Scholars have argued that "the main front where the future of the dollar will be decided is the global commodity market, especially the USD1.7 trillion oil market" (Luft, 2018). The use of nondollar currencies in global oil markets "is a serious challenge to the petrodollar system" (Foster, 2018). BRICS as a group is certainly strong enough to mount that challenge: in terms of consumption

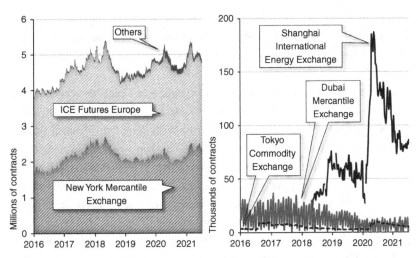

Figure 5 Leading global futures exchanges by crude oil contract open interest
Note: Shanghai International Energy Exchange series began on March 30, 2018. Open interest is the total number of futures contracts outstanding.
Source: Author compiled data from Bloomberg Financial.

power and forms a bigger oil-importing bloc than the entire European Union. China, the world's largest energy importer, and Russia, the world's largest energy exporter, are mobilizing within BRICS to promote "yuan oil futures," thereby challenging the US dollar's hegemonic position in the global oil market.

Following the 2018 BRICS Summit, China launched yuan oil futures, a renminbi-denominated oil futures contract, on the Shanghai International Energy Exchange. China's new oil futures are priced in renminbi, and renminbi is also convertible into gold on the Shanghai Gold Exchange and Hong Kong Gold Exchange.[13] This process has led to China, the world's largest oil importer, having an entirely domestic infrastructure for trading oil using gold, and that China's oil suppliers can receive payment in renminbi and immediately convert it into gold. This shift marks the beginning of a nondollar financial instrument and nondollar price discovering mechanism for a major global commodity. The Shanghai-traded yuan oil futures still lag behind rivals such as the London-traded Brent oil futures and the New York-traded WTI oil futures in terms of volume, but they have already surpassed comparable offerings traded in Tokyo and Dubai by a significant amount (Figure 5). The renminbi oil futures' accelerated growth has received the attention of leading central

---

[13] Yuan-denominated gold futures have been traded on the Shanghai Gold Exchange since April 2016 and on Hong Kong Gold Exchange since July 2017.

bankers in advanced economies. For example, Bank of England Governor Mark Carney (2019) observed that "the renminbi is now more common than sterling in oil future benchmarks, despite having no share in the market prior to 2018."

With the recent escalation of the US–China trade war, China has accelerated its promotion of a possible petroyuan, renminbi-denominated oil trading. In 2021, Chinese Foreign Minister Wang Yi went on a week-long tour of Saudi Arabia, Turkey, Iran, the UAE, Bahrain, and Oman. This trip was seen as a signal of China's intention to secure long-term energy deals with major Gulf energy producers to dictate oil pricing terms and fuel the rise of the petroyuan (Yeung, 2021). With China's push for the use of renminbi in oil pricing and trading and the strong global demand for a nondollar denominated oil trading mechanism, "the renminbi-denominated oil trading is likely to become more significant, partially displacing US dollar oil trading in one market after another" (Mathews and Selden, 2018). The prospect of a petroyuan would make it possible for countries under US sanctions, especially major oil exporters such as Iran and Russia, to access global markets via an alternative currency and nondollar payment systems, thereby weakening the effectiveness of US sanctions power.

China's primary motivation for promoting its yuan oil futures is to encourage the use of renminbi in oil trading and risk hedging, especially in the settling of physical oil deliveries to reduce exchange risks. The Chinese government cannot singlehandedly launch the yuan oil futures and ensure the fast growth in trading volume because commodities trading requires buyers and sellers. The fact that the yuan oil futures have been launched successfully and the trading volume has expanded indicates that there is great interest in the market to de-dollarize the global oil trade.

Russia also has a strong interest in de-dollarizing the global oil trade because major Russian energy companies have been under US sanctions since the Ukraine crisis in 2014. Being the world's largest oil and natural gas exporter, Russia's economic security revolves around vital oil and gas revenues. Oil and gas accounted for 60 percent of Russia's export revenues and nearly 40 percent of government revenues in 2017 (*Russian Matters*, 2018). BRICS supported Russia after the United States imposed sanctions on Russian companies. In June 2017, BRICS foreign ministers condemned "unilateral military intervention or economic sanctions in violation of international law and universally recognized norms of international relations" (China MOFA, 2017). China's launch of the yuan oil futures provides a crucial alternative trading platform for Russian oil companies and Russian oil consumers.

The potential of the yuan oil futures to advance global oil trade de-dollarization goes even further when considering the linkage to gold. China has sweetened the yuan oil futures by providing trading infrastructure to facilitate swapping oil into gold, with the renminbi serving as an intermediary funding step. If BRICS had their own pricing benchmark for gold – rather than being subject to London or New York's pricing – this infrastructure would potentially complete the goal of de-dollarizing the global oil trade, making it possible to trade oil using gold with minimum exposure to exchange risk. Sergey Shvetsov, the First Deputy Chairman of Russia's central bank confirmed in 2017 that BRICS countries were discussing the possibility of establishing a single gold trading system, both within BRICS and at the level of bilateral contracts (*TASS*, 2017). Shvetsov previously raised this theme at the bilateral level during his visit to China in 2016 (*TASS*, 2016). Such developments signal a potential BRICS alliance in the global physical gold market, where BRICS countries have major stakes: China, Russia, South Africa, and Brazil are major gold producers, and China and India are also the world's two largest gold consumers. A BRICS single gold trading system would facilitate the creation of a new gold pricing benchmark based upon global physical gold trading rather than gold derivatives. Combined with the gold-backed trading of yuan oil futures, oil producers could swap oil for gold rather than for US Treasury securities, further de-dollarizing the global oil market. Apart from de-dollarization, a BRICS single gold trading system would also help to strengthen domestic currency stability because it would free BRICS members from being subject to foreign pricing.

4.3 BRICS Alternatives to SWIFT and De-dollarizing Global Financial Infrastructure

In another effort to reduce their dependence on the US dollar, BRICS members have been building their own global payment infrastructures for international transactions that are independent of the US dollar and can serve as alternatives to SWIFT, the leading messaging network for financial transactions worldwide. This allows BRICS members, especially those who are often subjects of US sanctions, to create their own rules for international banking and settlement. Moreover, by extending alternative financial infrastructure to other countries and regions, BRICS can create greater buy-in for their own system and increase their financial and political influence through this alternative system.

Some BRICS members have independently developed their own cross-border payment mechanisms in recent years. Both Russia and China have launched their national alternatives to the SWIFT global banking network and introduced their systems to broader global markets. China's development of the renminbi cross-border payment system took place in the context of building the

BRI's financial infrastructure and renminbi internationalization. The added benefit of promoting broader use of the renminbi was to reduce foreign exchange risk and US sanctions risk for both China and its trading partners that may be under US sanctions, such as Iran or Russia. For Russia, establishing an international ruble payment system was the government's direct response to the heightened threat of Western sanctions since the Ukraine crisis in 2014. China and Russia recently established a direct payment settlement system with each other, with the intention to combine it with payment systems in other BRICS members and BRI countries in Eurasia. Russian officials also revealed that the other BRICS members would support the establishment of a common payment system at the BRICS level (Hamilton, 2019; *Reuters*, 2019c).

BRICS countries, with the exception of South Africa, have developed their own independent national payment systems, wholesale payment networks paired with a retail bank card network.[14] China and Russia have been leading the development of independent national payment systems, which are analyzed in more detail below as they might serve as building blocks for a larger BRICS-wide payment system or even one beyond BRICS in the future. An independent retail bank card network is a set of payment rails that establish protocols and procedures for the execution of retail payments and the exchange of related information among banks for final settlement over wholesale payment networks. An obvious benefit of having an independent retail bank card network, rather than relying upon leading American card network providers such as Visa or Mastercard, is to avoid the fees charged by these service providers. However, more importantly, if a country does not have its own payment rails and relies upon those of Visa or Mastercard – as pre-2014 Russia and pre-2002 China did, and as South Africa currently does – then those payment rails could be unilaterally withdrawn as a part of US sanctions. This withdrawal leaves domestic consumers without the ability to conduct basic retail transactions using bank cards. Connecting these national payment rails to an alternative cross-border payment system would allow the entire life cycle of payments to be carried out while entirely bypassing the US dollar-denominated global system.

4.3.1 China

Over the past decade, China has broadened the international coverage of the renminbi-based financial infrastructure featuring China's own cross-border payment system and UnionPay bank card network. China launched the Cross-Border Interbank Payment System (CIPS) for onshore renminbi clearance and

---

[14] South Africa so far does not have its own alternative to Visa or Mastercard, but it has been thinking about launching its own. For details, see *BusinessTech* (2021).

settlement services in 2015. The goal is to promote greater use of the renminbi and support renminbi internationalization. Within two years, CIPS' direct participants in terms of high-value payment reached 28, and its indirect participants reached 574, covering 85 countries and regions (*Xinhua*, 2017). By the end of 2020, the number of CIPS' direct participants reached a total of 43, and the number of indirect participants reached 1159, 867 of which were in Asia – including 522 Chinese mainland indirect participants – 147 in Europe, 26 in North America, 20 in Oceania, 17 in South America and 39 in Africa (CIPS World Service, 2020a). More than 3,000 banks and other financial institutions have conducted actual business through CIPS (CIPS World Service, 2020b). By the end of 2020, CIPS was processing RMB135.7 billion (USD19.4 billion) daily (*Reuters*, 2020). The annual business volume reached RMB45.3 trillion in 2020 (CIPS World Service, 2020b), despite the global economic slowdown caused by the COVID-19 pandemic.

CIPS allows global banks to clear cross-border renminbi transactions onshore directly instead of through offshore renminbi clearing banks. This empowers CIPS to serve as an alternative messaging system to SWIFT and thus reduce the risk of exposing transaction information to the United States, thereby mitigating the effect of US sanctions. However, CIPS has not yet departed from SWIFT. It currently uses SWIFT and its standards for cross-border financial messaging to connect with the global system. CIPS also adopted the ISO 2022 international payments messaging standard in order to make it interoperable with other payments systems as well as with correspondent banks around the world. The adoption of the existing cross-border messaging standards serves China's interest in making CIPS a critical piece of financial infrastructure to promote renminbi internationalization (SWIFT, 2016).

Nonetheless, the current close connections between CIPS and SWIFT do not negate the potential of the new infrastructure to break away from the existing US-dominated cross-border payment system because the adoption of the existing messaging standard fast-tracks the adoption of CIPS by global financial institutions. The more global participants there are in CIPS, the wider its direct communication with foreign financial institutions – and therefore, the larger its potential to operate independently. Moreover, the broader adoption of CIPS will also accelerate the wider use of the renminbi in the international financial system.

Although the renminbi has not yet become an international currency, UnionPay – China's central bank-approved independent bank card network launched in 2002 – has achieved a significant global presence. It has grown to be the largest supplier of bank payment cards, with over 7.5 billion cards issued worldwide, more than Visa and Mastercard combined (*UnionPay Media Reports*, 2019). UnionPay began to expand overseas in 2004 and quickly established a global payment network (Liu, 2016). By March 2021, the UnionPay acceptance network extended to 180 countries and regions, over half of which also accept UnionPay mobile payments, and more than 150 million UnionPay cards have been issued in 67 countries and regions outside Mainland China (UnionPay International, 2021). The globalization of UnionPay promotes the use of renminbi in cross-border settlements via outbound Chinese tourism consumption and international merchandise transactions.

UnionPay is widely accepted in all BRICS countries. In Brazil, UnionPay cards were first accepted at Brazilian ATMs in 2006. In March 2021, the acceptance rate of UnionPay bank cards reached 70 percent (Belt and Road Initiative, 2021). In Russia, UnionPay partnered with the Russian National Payments Card System in 2016, allowing both payment networks to accept UnionPay cards and Russian bank cards. This agreement broadened the international use of Russian bank cards (*China News*, 2016). UnionPay's acceptance rate in Russia reached over 90 percent in 2019 (*People's Daily*, 2019). UnionPay has also promoted its mobile payment feature in Russia. In 2018, UnionPay and Huawei jointly launched their Huawei Pay service in Russia, which was their first joint international market launch. In 2020, UnionPay partnered with Russia's Solidarnost Bank and Huawei to accelerate contactless payments in Russia and enable cardholders to use Huawei Pay on their Huawei or Honor smartphones (*Electronic Payments International*, 2020). Regarding India, in 2018, the Reserve Bank of India approved the cooperation between UnionPay and the National Payments Corporation of India, which runs the country's "RuPay" bank card network. This approval allowed UnionPay card holders to use all ATMs and point-of-sale terminals in India to withdraw cash or conduct transactions using the Indian rupee (Parmar, 2018). In December 2018, UnionPay cards were accepted at over 90 percent of ATMs in India (Pine Labs, 2018). South Africa's business with UnionPay started in 2008. Within a decade, UnionPay bank cards became widely accepted for withdrawal service by most ATMs of the four major South African banks. In 2019, the Standard Bank of South Africa launched its UnionPay cards in both virtual and physical form to local account holders to facilitate their payments in China (*Xinhua*, 2019). Besides working with local banks, UnionPay has also been working with retailers of all sizes in South Africa to enable their point-of-sale (POS) terminals at checkout counters across the country (*UnionPay Market News*, 2019). Overall, the growth of UnionPay in day-to-day transactions combined with the CIPS infrastructure gives China and other BRICS members an option to de-dollarize bilateral payments using renminbi as an alternative.

4.3.2 Russia

Russia's de-dollarization initiatives started in 2014 in the wake of US sanctions. Following Russia's annexation of Crimea, President Barack Obama signed Executive Order No. 13661, which targeted bank cards issued by seven Russian banks. Both Visa and Mastercard stopped processing transactions for their Russian customers, and about 500,000 credit cards and debit cards issued by these seven Russian banks found their payment function frozen (Xu, 2020). This severely affected Russia's domestic and international economic exchanges. Moreover, the United States and the United Kingdom also threatened to cut off Russia from SWIFT. In this context, Russia began building two pieces of financial infrastructure that are critical for reducing its exposure to US sanctions, namely (1) an independent national payment system to serve as Russia's alternative to Visa or Mastercard and (2) a proprietary financial messaging system as Russia's equivalent to SWIFT.

Russia's de-dollarization of financial infrastructure started when the Russian State Duma passed the National Payment Card System (NSPK) Act in 2014. This Act established the National Payment Card System Joint Stock Company as the main operation and settlement center of the NSPK, which was owned by Russia's central bank. In July 2015, through public tender in Russia, the card was named "MIR," which means both "world" and "peace" in Russian. By August 2017, more than 13.9 million MIR cards had been issued in Russia (representing 10 percent of the Russian population). By the first half of 2019, 312 banks in Russia had joined the system. Practically all trade and service points, including cafes, shops, restaurants, and petrol stations, now accept payments with MIR cards. MIR cards are also welcomed in sanctions-hit Crimea, where Western banks have been prohibited from operating. MIR's performance shows other governments how to challenge established payments giants based in the United States, such as Visa and Mastercard.

Since 2014, Russia has also been developing its own proprietary financial messaging system called "System for Transfer of Financial Messages" (SPFS) as the Russian analog to SWIFT. It can be connected to both foreign banks and foreign legal entities. According to the director of the Bank of Russia's national payment system Alla Bakina, 8 foreign banks and 34 legal entities signed agreements to join the SPFS by 2019 (Chaudhury, 2019b). Traffic through the system has been growing and accounted for around 15 percent of all internal traffic in 2019, up from 10 to 11 percent in 2018

(Chaudhury, 2019b). Moreover, Russia has been actively seeking to expand SPFS's international presence. Opening up SPFS to foreign banks was part of President Putin's agenda to further undermine the US dollar after his election victory in 2018. In 2019, Russia and Iran connected their financial messaging systems, linking banks in both countries through SPFS and SEPAM (the Iranian alternative to SWIFT) (*Financial Tribune*, 2019). Russia also introduced SPFS to banks in the Eurasian Economic Union (EEU) region (*Russia Briefing*, 2019). The same year, Russian Finance Minister Anton Siluanov signed an agreement with Turkey to start using the ruble and the lira in cross-border payments and settlements, greatly increasing the possibility of connecting Turkish banks and companies to SPFS and using Russian MIR cards in Turkey (*Reuters*, 2019b). Besides the EEU region and Turkey, Russia also expressed interest in linking SPFS with other countries in the Middle East and European region (Chaudhury 2019b; *Reuters*, 2019a; *Russia Business Today*, 2019).

4.3.3 A Potential "China-Russia Plus" Coalition to Create a SWIFT Alternative

Russia has sought to mobilize its BRICS partners, particularly China, to achieve wider acceptance of its MIR card system and greater international coverage of its SPFS infrastructure. In November 2016, Prime Minister Medvedev said that Russia desired a mutually compatible payments system with China that would harmonize the two countries' national payment systems to preemptively deal with the risk of being cut off from SWIFT (Soldatkin, 2016). He also said that Russia and China discussed the launch of a new cross-border payment system for direct trade invoices settlements in renminbi and ruble. Medvedev made it clear that this initiative was an attempt to move away from the current dollar-dominated financial system and bypass Western sanctions (Rolfe, 2018). In June 2019, Russia and China agreed to deepen cooperation in national payment card systems and cross-border payments in national currencies (*TASS Russian News Agency*, 2019). In March 2021, Russian Foreign Minister Sergei Lavrov again called for China to work with Russia to reduce their dependence on the US dollar and Western payment systems and push back against the West's "ideological agenda" (Osborn, 2021).

On China's side, the PBoC has improved the efficiency of transactions between the two national currencies. In October 2017, the PBoC approved the China Foreign Exchange Trading System (CFETS) to institute a payment versus payment (PVP) system to facilitate financial transactions between renminbi and ruble. This PVP system can shorten the delivery time lag between the two currencies from at least a day to only a few seconds, which is a major improvement in transaction efficiency and will greatly reduce foreign exchange transaction risk (PRC Gov., 2017). This PVP system was the very first of its kind. Its launch marked the official establishment of a PVP mechanism for transactions between renminbi and foreign currencies in China's foreign exchange market.

India was reported to have expressed interest in jointly exploring an alternative to SWIFT with Russia and China in order to conduct trade with countries under US sanctions (Chaudhury, 2019b). While India currently does not have its own domestic financial messaging system, it has plans to link a service that is currently under development with Russia's SPFS, which could possibly be linked with China's CIPS. Once this is materialized, this linked system would cover most parts of the world (Hillman, 2020, p. 5).

4.3.4 A Common BRICS Payment System and BRICS Digital Currency

A collective and perhaps more ambitious step toward de-dollarization is the "BRICS Pay" system currently under development. It is a single contactless payment system that connects BRICS' national payment systems with an integrated cloud platform for payment. BRICS Pay will not duplicate the national payment systems that are already in place in the member countries; rather, the system leverages the latest fintech innovations in BRICS countries to integrate BRICS members' individual payment systems. BRICS Pay will link the credit or debit cards of BRICS citizens to online wallets, which will be accessible 24/7 for payment via a mobile application installed on their smartphones. The BRICS Pay system is part of BRICS' collective effort to establish a common system for retail payments and transactions between its members. However, BRICS is willing to expand its scope, and non-BRICS countries will also be able to use the platform. The pilot project kicked off in South Africa in early April 2019. In 2020, the Russian BRICS Presidency proposed the idea of a commercial "BRICS Pay" for "BRICS Plus" countries for the consideration of the BRICS Business Council (BRICS Business Council, 2020, p. 67).

The biggest advantage of BRICS Pay is that this proposed integrated payment system would make possible the use of BRICS members' national currencies as a direct basis of exchange for external payments. Currently, external settlements between BRICS members still require a conversion into US dollars, which requires the engagement of US banks. For example, a yuan-ruble non-cash settlement using UnionPay cannot happen directly; it must be converted into US dollars first. Through BRICS Pay, the conversion to US dollar and US banks would no longer be necessary because payments would be settled using the national currencies of the BRICS members. The BRICS Pay system will also allow the members to reduce their dependence on international payment organizations such as SWIFT, Visa, and Mastercard. It could potentially give BRICS members a shared competitive advantage to compete with traditional banks in the global financial services market, currently dominated by US banks, as well as US rules and norms. The integrated BRICS Pay system connecting the national payment systems of BRICS members while also allowing non-BRICS countries to participate could potentially disrupt the financial dominance of the incumbent Western global financial powerhouses. Russia has expressed that the foundation of a new international payment system is a priority for BRICS as a group which is driven by "increasing non-market risks of the global payment infrastructure" (*Banks am*, 2019; *Moscow Times*, 2019b).

Building a common framework for BRICS Pay is the BRICS' attempt toward de-dollarization through the conventional route of promoting local fiat currencies in cross-border settlements. Meanwhile, BRICS has also been exploring an unconventional route toward this end: the use of blockchain technology to build a BRICS digital currency. During the BRICS Xiamen Summit in 2017, the BRICS Finance Committee discussed the possibility of replacing the US dollar with a BRICS cryptocurrency in settlements among members (*RT International*, 2017). At the 2018 BRICS Summit, BRICS countries' development banks signed an agreement to cooperate on blockchain research and digital economy development, thereby working on frontier technological developments together (Vnesheconombank, 2018). They agreed to form a joint research working group, set a research agenda, and carry out research toward identifying potential applications of blockchain technology in the financial sector, particularly in infrastructure financing (Srivats, 2018). The 2019 BRICS Summit further prioritized the bloc's cooperation in blockchain and digital economy (Chaudhury, 2019a). The BRICS Business Council supported the idea of creating a single payment system for settlements between BRICS members during this summit. As the head of the Russian Direct Investment Fund Kirill Dmitriev pointed out, an efficiently operating BRICS payment system can facilitate settlements in national currencies and ensure the stability of settlements and investments among BRICS, which form more than 20 percent of the global influx of foreign direct investment (*Reuters*, 2019c). A BRICS cryptocurrency could be integrated into the common BRICS payment framework, and it would take the form of a paperless document flow to facilitate transactions. Given that BRICS members have agreed upon blockchain R&D cooperation, it is possible for them to develop this system using blockchain technology (Palmer, 2019; RBC, 2019).

Apart from discussing the prospect of a shared BRICS cryptocurrency, BRICS members have been developing their own central bank digital currency (CBDC) that could potentially revolutionize the global currency system. China started its CBDC project in 2014 and revealed its strategic agenda in 2016 (People's Bank of China, 2016). Since 2020, China has launched the "Digital Currency Electronic Payment" program in several Chinese cities, including Shenzhen. In 2021, cross-border tests of digital renminbi were conducted in Hong Kong with the Hong Kong Monetary Authority. Since then, there have been discussions regarding the broadening and deepening of the use of digital renminbi. The rollout of digital renminbi payment infrastructure in Hong Kong could increase the speed of cross-border payment and clearing processes while also cutting costs.[15] Some US experts have raised concerns that digital renminbi would present the opportunity to bypass the global bank-based system and allow China to make direct payments to other countries, diminishing the impact of US sanctions (Nelson, 2021). In light of such concerns, Deputy Governor of the PBoC Li Bo responded that China's digital renminbi is aimed at domestic use rather than to replace the US dollar (*Bloomberg News*, 2021).

Other BRICS members have also been exploring their options for CBDC. According to Roberto Campos Neto, President of Brazil's central bank, Brazil may be ready for a CBDC as early as 2022 (Nelson, 2020). The Central Bank of Brazil has already done some groundwork and laid critical infrastructure for the issuance of a CBDC. In 2020, it launched its own blockchain platform called PIER (Platform for Information Integration of Regulatory Entities), which allows for the exchange of data between financial regulatory authorities (Central Bank of Brazil, 2020). It also launched a 24/7 instant payment system called "PIX" to improve the efficiency and competitiveness of the retail payment market in Brazil (Ayres, Mandl, and McGeever, 2020). It was reported that "PIX" supports peer-to-peer and business-to-business transactions in 10 seconds or less via mobile phone, internet banking, and select ATMs (Haig, 2020).

Russia has also fast-tracked its national digital currency development. Elvira Nabiullina, Governor of Russia's central bank, referred to digital currency as "the future for our financial system because it correlates with the development of digital economy" (Shead, 2021). In 2020, Russia's central bank outlined Russia's plan for a digital ruble, aiming to launch a pilot program at the end of 2021 (Bank of Russia, 2020; Shome, 2021). As of October 2020, at least five

---

[15] It was estimated that costs related to cross-border payments in Hong Kong are about USD 20 billion to USD 40 billion per year, the equivalent of about 11 percent of the city's GDP in 2020. If the e-CNY payment infrastructure were to roll out for cross-border payment at scale, it could address a substantial portion of this cost paseo. For more details, see Ekberg and Ho (2021).

Russian banks had expressed interest in participating in future, non-public tests of the digital ruble (Partz, 2020).

South Africa has been interested in the prospect of its own CBDC.[16] The South African Reserve Bank has been conducting research on CBDC since late 2016.[17] It successfully completed a 14-week proof-of-concept trial for "Project Khokha" (Khokha means 'pay' in the South African Zulu language), testing the idea of a commercial payment system for interbank settlement using a tokenized South African rand on Ethereum-based blockchain Quorum (*BitcoinAfrica*, 2018; Groepe, 2018; Tobor 2018). The test results showed that "the typical daily volume of the South African payments system could be processed in less than two hours with full confidentiality of transactions and settlement finality" (South African Reserve Bank, 2018). The central bank launched "Project Khokha 2" in February 2021 to explore the use of both a wholesale CBDC and a wholesale privately issued settlement token for interbank settlement (Intergovernmental Fintech Working Group, 2021).

Following China's launch of the digital renminbi, the Indian government proposed to prohibit all private cryptocurrencies and create a framework for an official digital currency in February 2021 (Ghosh, 2021). In 2018, the Reserve Bank of India (2018) announced that it had constituted a team to study the desirability and feasibility of a CBDC. According to Governor Shaktikanta Das, the Reserve Bank of India has been preparing to launch its own digital currency (Ghosh, 2021).

At the current stage, none of the alternative payment systems discussed above has achieved truly global status, with the exception of China's UnionPay network. However, the proliferation of these substitutes shows that BRICS members are eager to take defensive measures and build their own versions of financial infrastructures to sanction-proof their international transactions.

4.4 BRICS Plus: De-dollarization Mobilization beyond BRICS

The BRICS countries have leveraged their overlapping memberships in other non-Western multilateral institutions to build wider coalitions around their "go-it-alone" de-dollarization initiatives. Annual BRICS summits have been a convenient platform for such mobilization. For example, EEU and SCO members and observers were invited to the 2015 BRICS Summit to gain their support for de-dollarization efforts. During this meeting, Chinese President Xi

---

[16] Interview with a former official at South Africa's National Treasury, January 7, 2021. Interview with a senior economist at the SARB February 3, 2021, and interview with a researcher at a South African think tank, January 12, 2021.

[17] Interview with a senior economist at the SARB, February 3, 2021.

emphasized that the BRICS, the SCO, and the EEU are all influential mechanisms of cooperation and that the gathering of state leaders sent out a positive signal of unity and cooperation to emerging markets and other developing countries (China MOFA, 2015). In 2017, the BRICS leaders, together with the leaders of Egypt, Guinea, Tajikistan, Mexico, and Thailand, held the "Dialogue of Emerging Market and Developing Countries" on the margins of the BRICS Xiamen Summit (*People's Daily*, 2017). This dialogue marked the launch of the China-initiated "BRICS Plus." BRICS Plus expands the BRICS platform to bring in other countries and regional integration institutions, such as the Mercosur, the SCO, EEU, South African Customs Union, South Asian Association for Regional Cooperation, and ASEAN + China. BRICS Plus brings together thirty-five countries to form an expanded platform that can coordinate policies with BRICS' regional partners across the four continents. As such, it provides a convenient venue for de-dollarization policy coordination and nondollar financial infrastructure construction.

A notable example of broader mobilization through the BRICS Plus informal institution is a sub-group of the BRICS Plus, namely, the SCO. Several BRICS members are members of the SCO – both China and Russia are founding members, and India joined as a full member in 2017. With three of the five BRICS members being also SCO members, it is likely that these two non-Western institutions will conduct policy sharing and policy coordination through both platforms, including policies designed to reduce their dependence on the US dollar. The SCO was initially established for security cooperation, but it has gradually taken on economic dimensions as well. Before the Shanghai summit in 2006, SCO members launched the "SCO Mechanism of Interbank Cooperation." During the Shanghai Summit, members also launched the SCO Business Council to facilitate greater economic cooperation within the SCO framework (Shanghai Cooperation Organization, 2006). BRICS has initiated similar efforts, launching the BRICS Interbank Cooperation Mechanism in 2010 and the BRICS Business Council in 2013. In 2020, the SCO announced plans to further enhance financial cooperation and expressed willingness to continue discussions on the establishment of the SCO Development Bank and the SCO Development Fund. The SCO members underscored the importance of joint approaches to the use of national currencies in mutual settlements between interested SCO member states (*Xinhua*, 2020). The development of SCO financial cooperation initiatives suggests that China, India, and Russia can potentially introduce de-dollarization policies in the SCO and achieve synergies with similar initiatives in BRICS policy platforms.

The SCO's consideration of launching its own development bank suggests a BRICS-like path: building formal institutions that can promote the use of local currencies in BRICS' development finance and reduce risks associated with US dollar financing. The convergence in institutional arrangement and mandates between the SCO and BRICS set the foundation for closer economic and financial policy cooperation between them. Such similarities can provide formal channels for further policy coordination between these two developing-country coalitions on issues such as: expanding the scale and scope of bilateral currency swaps, promoting the use of local currencies in cross-border trade and investment, and eventually reducing the countries' dependence on the US dollar. In fact, closer alignment between BRICS and SCO toward de-dollarization has already been taking place. SCO Secretary-General Vladimir Norov recently confirmed that the SCO members have been working on a gradual transition to mutual settlements in national currencies, with representatives of the SCO Interbank Consortium already engaged in this activity. He also raised the need for the SCO to establish partnerships with the AIIB, the NDB, and the Silk Road Fund to fully unlock the investment potential of the SCO (*TASS*, 2021). In 2020, SCO Finance Ministers agreed to send recommendations to finalize a roadmap to promote bilateral trade and investments and issue bonds using local currencies.

To summarize the findings of this section, we have demonstrated that BRICS and its members have pursued de-dollarization through the "go-it-alone" strategy using both institutional and market mechanisms to achieve greater autonomy and influence. The specific examples of the NDB and development finance de-dollarization, BRICS commitments to develop a BRICS alternative to SWIFT, and the members' joint vision for a BRICS digital currency suggest that BRICS has demonstrated a high level of coalitional strength in executing high-effectiveness de-dollarization initiatives. These are club goods that could serve as critical elements for developing an alternative nondollar global financial system and help shield members from the dollar volatility and US sanction risk. Moreover, there are also powerful sub-coalitional dynamics at play. De-dollarization initiatives at the sub-BRICS level have been most active, with Russia and China being the two pivotal states leading these "go-it-alone" initiatives. A Russia–China de-dollarization mini-coalition is emerging, with the potential for broader participation by other countries under US sanctions, such as Iran. Deteriorating US–China relations will very likely drive China to move closer to Russia and double down on de-dollarization in the future. Additionally, BRICS has also attempted to create broader coalitions by leveraging the members' overlapping memberships in other non-Western organizations, such as the use of BRICS Plus and its engagement with SCO and EEU. Although such broader mobilization has not yet yielded significant tangible results and has not led to any broader de-dollarization public goods, BRICS has certainly demonstrated its leadership as the rule maker and agenda setter for promoting the use of local currencies in international trade and finance, compatible with the goal to achieve higher international influence.

Currently, predominantly Russia and China's "go-it-alone" de-dollarization initiatives are unlikely to liberate the BRICS members from the dollar-based global financial system any time soon because of three major constraints. First, the limited capacity of the NDB means BRICS cannot achieve full de-dollarization in international borrowing for development finance. All BRICS members have been strongly in favor of promoting local currency development financing through the NDB, but the NDB's capacity is much more limited relative to traditional development financiers such as the World Bank or the Asian Development Bank. While the NDB has been considering potential expansion, its size and scope constrain BRICS collective de-dollarization potential. Second, not all BRICS members have the resources or capacity to sponsor their own market infrastructures or instruments. Now only China and Russia have political incentives and the capacity to develop their own alternatives to SWIFT and seek to connect them. Moreover, only China's market size is large and influential enough to launch an alternative oil futures contract, like the yuan oil futures, to the US dollar market. Thus, it is currently unlikely that the BRICS members would completely abandon the US dollar-based financial infrastructure. Third, the internal geopolitical dynamics within BRICS and its members' relationships with the United States may prevent BRICS from formally making the group a de-dollarization advocacy coalition, which would be the fastest way to implement the "go-it-alone" strategy and gain followers.

5 "Reform-the-Status-Quo" Strategy: Remaking Existing Institutions and Markets

Besides "go-it-alone" initiatives, BRICS countries have also pursued de-dollarization through a "reform-the-status-quo" strategy to dilute the US dollar's dominance in the *existing* global financial system. To this end, BRICS members have diversified their reserve assets at the individual state level and have also collectively built an internal layer of support through the dollar-based CRA to modify their dependence on the IMF. BRICS also jointly negotiated the reform of the IMF SDR. BRICS' stock exchanges have also formed an alliance that has been reshaping global equity markets. Such BRICS-level initiatives demonstrate BRICS' strength as a de-dollarization coalition working within the existing dollar-based system to improve BRICS

autonomy and influence. At the sub-BRICS level, members have been promoting the use of local currencies in bilateral trade and strengthening internal
currency cooperation by using bilateral currency swaps to diffuse the US
dollar's dominance as the vehicle currency. These sub-BRICS initiatives do
not directly improve the global influence of the members, but they help
achieve the goal of greater autonomy by reducing exchange risk in bilateral
trade and reducing the risk of US sanctions.

5.1 Strengthening Self-Defense Against the Dollar's Dominance

An important aspect of the US dollar's supremacy is the established tradition of
using US Treasury securities as the proxy for risk-free assets in global financial
markets. Many central banks and sovereign institutional investors hold their
reserves and other financial assets in US Treasury securities because of their
nearly risk-free nature and credible liquidity. BRICS central banks and sovereign investors are no exception. Having a concentrated portfolio of US Treasury
securities has not only increased the opportunity costs for the BRICS members
in times of a weakening US dollar, but it has also increased their geopolitical
vulnerability to US sanctions. To strengthen their self-defense against the US
dollar hegemony, major BRICS central banks, especially the Bank of Russia,
have diversified their reserve assets by reducing their holdings of US Treasury
securities. Moreover, BRICS also established CRA as a pooled US dollar
reserve and an internal first line of defense to help members during small-
scale balance of payments shortfalls. All of these measures allow BRICS
members to strengthen their self-defense against volatilities in the US dollar
and improve their internal support for liquidity in times of dollar shortages.

Russia has been the most aggressive among BRICS in substituting US dollar
reserves with alternative reserve assets. Since 2013, the Bank of Russia has been
trying to reduce the number of transactions conducted in US dollars and has
increased the use of euros, renminbi, and rubles in settlements. In April 2018,
following a new round of stringent US sanctions on Russia, the Bank changed
the structure of its reserve assets, reducing the dollar's share in favor of the yuan
and the euro. It also expedited the withdrawal of its reserves out of US Treasury
bonds. US Treasury International Capital (TIC) data showed that Russian
holdings of Treasury securities declined by 84 percent between March and
May 2018, falling from USD96.1 billion to USD14.9 billion in just two months
(Figure 6). In early 2019, the Bank of Russia revealed that it reduced US dollar
holdings by USD101 billion – over half of its existing US dollar assets. For
comparison, in February 2013, before Russia's annexation of Crimea, Russian
investments in US Treasury bonds stood at USD164.3 billion. After the Biden

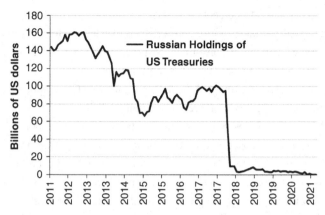

Figure 6 Russian holdings of US treasuries (2006–2021, USD billions)
Note: Includes both short- and long-term US Treasury obligations.
Sources: Author compiled data from US Department of the Treasury (2021) data on major foreign holders of Treasury securities.

administration imposed new sanctions on Russia for cyberattacks and election interference in April 2021, Russia accelerated the pace of de-dollarizing its reserve assets (Macias and Turak, 2021). Russia decided to completely remove dollar assets from its National Wealth Fund (NWF), whose portfolio forms part of Russia's currency and gold reserves and had a value of USD186 billion by the end of May 2021 (Kantchev, 2021; Shead, 2021).

Renminbi was one of the biggest beneficiaries of the de-dollarization of Russian reserves. In early 2019, Russia's central bank invested USD44 billion into renminbi, increasing its share in Russia's foreign exchange reserves from 5 percent to 15 percent (Simes, 2020). Russia's renminbi holdings are about ten times the global average for central banks, accounting for about a quarter of global renminbi reserves (Andrianova and Doff, 2019). With NWF's ongoing de-dollarization, this number is likely to increase. In 2021, the Kremlin allowed Russia's sovereign wealth fund to invest in renminbi and Chinese state bonds. Russia's aggressive de-dollarization policies are conducive to strengthening a potential Russia–China partnership for de-dollarization. Russian experts have suggested that Russia's push to accumulate renminbi is not just about diversifying reserves but also about encouraging China to become more assertive in challenging US global economic leadership (Simes, 2020).

Besides replacing US dollar reserves with other currencies, the Bank of Russia has also been implementing a gold strategy to move away from US assets. It has been the largest buyer of gold in the past few years, quadrupling Russia's gold reserves over the past decade: between 2018 and 2019, the value of Russia's gold reserves increased by 42 percent, to USD109.5 billion (*Moscow Times*, 2019a). As a result, gold has taken up the largest share of Russia's total reserves since 2000. By June 2020, gold constituted 23 percent of the reserves of Russia's central bank, while the share of US dollar assets declined to 22 percent. Russia's gold strategy has made it the leader among BRICS members measured by the percentage of gold in total reserves (Figures 7–9).

The BRICS CRA helps further strengthen BRICS collective defense against balance of payments crises due to US dollar shortages. BRICS members are allowed to draw from the CRA's collective pool of USD100 billion reserves through swaps using their own currencies in times of need (BRICS, 2014). Some scholars view the CRA as an institution that challenges the IMF, especially in light of BRICS' dissatisfaction with the conditionalities of IMF lending and the domination of Western powers in the IMF (e.g., Roberts, Armijo and Katada, 2017). Yet the CRA remains dependent on the IMF, and it cannot serve as a substitute for the IMF. Only 30 percent of accessible CRA funds are available to BRICS members on demand, whereas accessing the remaining 70 percent requires arrangements with the IMF.[18] This provisional dependence on the IMF preserves the sustainability of the CRA's pooled US dollar reserves. If the maximum amount is insufficient, then BRICS members would resort to the IMF. This establishes an internal first line of defense for BRICS members up to the authorized amount. Thus, the CRA modifies BRICS dependence on IMF's rescuing mechanisms by adding an additional layer of defense and acts *within and conditional upon* the existing dollar-based system while strengthening BRICS' self-defense against a US dollar shortage.

5.2 Reforming the Global Reserve Currency Structure

The BRICS members have collectively attempted to disrupt the US dollar's dominant position in the current global reserve currency structure through promoting the reform of the IMF's SDR and supporting the renminbi's inclusion into the SDR basket. These initiatives are part of the BRICS' broader efforts to reform the existing multilateral international financial institutions.

Chinese officials had expressed China's interest in restructuring the global reserves currency structure and advocated for giving the SDR a greater role several months before the first BRIC summit. In March 2009, the PBoC

---

[18] This is specified in the CRA's rationale document: "Where financing in excess of this 30 percent limit is required, an 'IMF-linked portion' will be made available. This will allow the country access to the remaining 70 percent provided that a conditionality-based agreement with the IMF is concluded." China can request up to half its commitment (USD41 billion) from this total, Russia, India, and Brazil can request up to its USD18 billion commitment, and South Africa can request twice its contribution at USD10 billion. For more details, see BRICS (2014). See also Biziwick, Cattaneo and Fryer (2015).

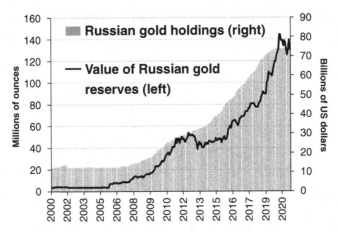

Figure 7 Russia's increasing gold reserves

Sources: Central Bank of Russian Federation, International Reserves of the Russian Federation.

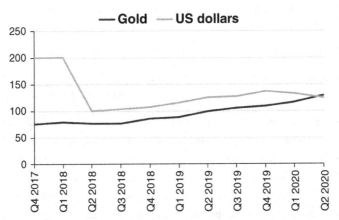

Figure 8 Russia's gold reserves vs. dollar reserves as of June 2020

Sources: Bank of Russia (2021), International Reserves of the Russian Federation.

Governor, Zhou Xiaochuan, called for making the SDR into a "super-sovereign reserve currency" (Zhou, 2009). Later, the United Nations (UN) echoed Zhou's idea and proposed establishing a new Global Reserve System based on the IMF's SDR. The UN proposal stated:

> [t]he global imbalances which played an important role in this crisis can only be addressed if there is a better way of dealing with international economic risks facing countries than the current system of accumulating international reserves. ... To resolve this problem a new Global Reserve System, what may be viewed as a greatly expanded SDR, with regular or cyclically adjusted

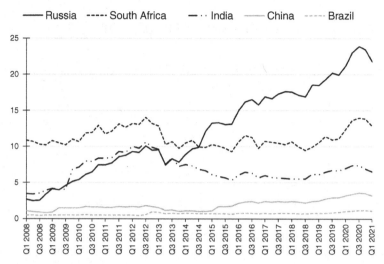

Figure 9 BRICS Central Banks reserves (percent of gold as total reserves, Q1 2008–Q1 2021)

Sources: Central banks, ICE Benchmark Administration, International Monetary Fund, World Gold Council.

emissions calibrated to the size of reserve accumulations, could contribute to global stability, economic strength, and global equity

(UN General Assembly, 2009).

Russia showed its support for this proposal within a week and stated that Russia and China "have similar positions" on the reform of the international financial system (*Xinhua*, 2009). In June 2009, days before the BRIC summit, President Dmitry Medvedev expressed Russia's dissatisfaction with the existing reserve currency structure and called upon the IMF to expand the SDR basket to include the renminbi, commodity currencies such as the ruble, and gold to create a supranational reserve currency for international settlements (Doman-b 2009; Wang, 2009). Russia raised this issue again during the first BRIC summit (Bryanski, 2009) and revealed its plan to reduce the share of US Treasury bills in its USD400 billion reserves. This sentiment resonated with China and Brazil's decision to invest USD40 billion and USD10 billion, respectively, in IMF bonds, with another USD10 billion from India (Kelly, 2009; Stuenkel, 2014). In this context, the issue of reforming the global reserve currency structure has become an important issue for BRICS, and members have shown their collective commitment to diversifying their reserves away from being overly concentrated in US dollar assets.

The 2011 BRICS Summit highlighted BRICS members' shared interests in reforming the existing reserve currency structure. BRICS leaders declared that they "support the reform and improvement of the international monetary system, with a broad-based international reserve currency system providing stability and certainty ... and welcome the current discussion about the role of the SDR in the existing international monetary system including the composition of SDR basket of currencies" (BRICS, 2011). During the 2013 BRICS Summit, BRICS members reiterated their commitment to reforming and diversifying the global monetary structure, using almost the same language that they used in 2011 (BRICS, 2013). BRICS members also jointly expressed their support for the inclusion of renminbi into the SDR basket in October 2016 in their Goa Declaration (BRICS, 2016).

BRICS' efforts to reform the existing system have thus far led to limited success. BRICS combined voting rights at the World Bank and IMF and BRICS total SDR quota are all below 15 percent of total (Table 5). These numbers are still misaligned with BRICS' collective economic power, which represents close to a quarter of global GDP. This limited success indicates the mounting difficulty facing BRICS members to further advance their voice and representation in the existing global system. If reforming the system from the inside becomes unlikely, BRICS may resort to "go-it-alone" strategies.

5.3 Diffusing the Dollar's Dominance as the Vehicle Currency in Trade

BRICS members are keen to promote the use of their national currencies in trade settlements, and they have discussed this issue at BRICS summits for nearly two decades (see Section 3). High-level agreements on trade de-dollarization, as expressed in BRICS joint statements, have materialized through bilateral agreements among the members. For example, in June 2009, China and Russia reached an agreement to move toward settling bilateral trade in local currencies (Vorobyova, 2009). A few days later, China and Brazil also announced an "initial understanding" to gradually eliminate the US dollar in their bilateral trade, which was estimated to be USD40 billion at that time (*MercoPress*, 2009). During the 2013 BRICS Summit, India's Commerce and Industry Minister, Anand Sharma, discussed his proposal to settle bilateral payments in local currencies with his South African counterpart Rob Davies (Dilasha, 2013). In 2015, South Africa's Investec Bank and the China Export-Import Bank acted on this proposal and signed a Strategic Cooperation Agreement, which included the use of renminbi as a settlement currency in trade. In June 2016, the PBoC added the South African rand, allowing for direct trading on the Chinese interbank market (*EIU ViewsWire*, 2016).

To further promote the use of local currencies in bilateral trade, the BRICS members augmented their agreements through a series of bilateral currency swaps, especially between China and other BRICS members. In 2013, the new

Table 5 BRICS representation in major global multilateral institutions

Country	World Bank		IDA		MIGA		IMF		SDR Quota	
	No. of votes	% of total	No. of votes	% of total	No. of votes	% of total	No. of votes	% of total	Millions	% of total
Brazil	54,264	2.11	477,996	1.66	2,830	1.3	111,878	2.22	11,042.00	2.32
Russia	67,260	2.62	90,647	0.31	5,752	2.64	130,495	2.59	12,903.70	2.71
India	76,777	2.99	835,156	2.89	1,218	0.56	132,602	2.63	13,114.40	2.76
China	131,426	5.11	660,966	2.29	5,754	2.64	306,287	6.08	30,482.90	6.41
South Africa	18,698	0.73	74,369	0.26	1,886	0.86	31,970	0.63	3,051.20	0.64
Total	348,425	13.56	2,139,134	7.41	17,440	8	713,232	14.15	70,594.20	14.84

IDAL, International Development Association; MIGA, Multilateral Investment Guarantee Agency

Source: Author compiled data from World Bank, IDA, MIGA, and IMF.

China-Brazil bilateral swap agreement allowed them to trade in local currencies in the equivalent of up to USD30 billion per year, which accounted for half of the bilateral trade between the two countries in 2012 (Lopes and Flak, 2013). In 2014, Russia and China signed a three-year currency swap deal worth RMB 150 billion (USD24.5 billion) (*Reuters*, 2014). This was extended for another three years in 2017 (Simes, 2020). In 2015, South Africa and China signed a three-year bilateral swap agreement worth 57 billion rand (USD4.75 billion) (*Reuters*, 2015). Apart from this 2015 agreement, BRICS' bilateral currency swaps have mostly been in renminbi. This is unsurprising given that renminbi is the most internationalized of all BRICS' national currencies.

BRICS' efforts toward de-dollarization in international trade have progressed, especially in bilateral trade. Between 2013 and 2019, the use of local currency in India–Russia bilateral trade increased from 6 percent to 30 percent (Chaudhury and Pubby, 2019). According to Andrey Denisov, the Russian Ambassador to China, about 25 percent of bilateral trade between Russia and China was settled using local currencies in 2020, which was about a nine-fold growth over less than seven years. In comparison, the use of local currencies in their bilateral trade was about 2–3 percent during 2013 and 2014 (China MOFCOM, 2021). The use of renminbi in trade in South Africa grew 65 percent in 2016 (Danese, 2016). The bilateral currency swaps also proved useful for circumventing US sanctions. Under stringent sanctions in 2014, the bilateral currency swap between Russian and Chinese central banks enabled Russia to circumvent Western isolation and fostered a de-dollarization dynamic between China and Russia (Antoniades, 2017). Between October 2015 and March 2016, Russia used these swap lines multiple times to support bilateral trade and direct investment between Russia and China (McDowell, 2019).

At the BRICS country level, Russia has achieved the greatest reduction in the use of the US dollar in its trade since 2013. Russia's trade de-dollarization hit a milestone by the fourth quarter of 2020 when the share of its exports sold in US dollars fell below 50 percent for the first time. However, the decline of the US dollar was not replaced by the ruble but rather picked up by the euro. The share of euro used in Russia's export transactions increased to 36.1 percent, contrasting with a mere 8.7 percent in the first quarter of 2013 (Figure 10).

Bilateral trade de-dollarization within BRICS has progressed most rapidly in Russia–China trade. This has been catalyzed by the increasing use of local currencies in Russia's exports to China, especially after major Russian energy companies stopped using the US dollar in their energy exports. For example, in 2015, Gazprom Neft announced that it settled all of its oil exports to China in renminbi (Du, 2015; Farchy, 2015). The rise of the euro in Russia–China trade also accelerated in 2019, when Russia's top crude oil producer, Rosneft,

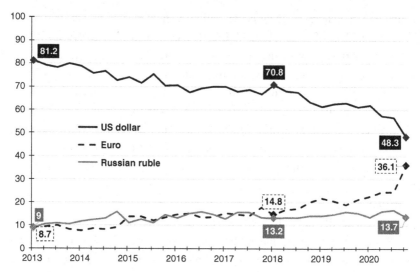

Figure 10 Declining use of the dollar in Russia's export transactions since 2013 (percent, 2013–2020)

Source: Author compiled data from Bloomberg Financial and Bank of Russia.

switched all export contracts to euros from US dollars to protect itself from intensifying US sanctions (Aliaj and Astrasheuskaya, 2019). By the end of 2020, more than 83 percent of Russian exports to China were settled in euro (Figure 11). The euro has now replaced the US dollar and has become the primary vehicle currency in Russia–China trade.

As their relations with the United States have both worsened in recent years, Russia and China have moved closer to jointly de-dollarize bilateral trade and promoting the use of local currencies in trade settlements. In 2018, President Putin announced that "the Russian and Chinese sides confirmed their interest in using national currencies more actively in reciprocal payments" (*Deutsche Welle*, 2018). In 2019, following his meeting with President Xi, Putin confirmed that Russia and China "intend to develop the practice of settlements in national currencies" (*RT International*, 2019a). Meanwhile, Russia and China signed a joint declaration announcing the elevation of their bilateral relationship to the level of "comprehensive strategic partnership of coordination for a new era" (PRC Gov., 2019). This upgrade in their relationship enables China and Russia to ramp up their collective efforts to reduce dependence on the US dollar. Concurrent with this upgrade in bilateral relations, Russian Finance Minister Anton Siluanov and the PBoC Governor Yi Gang signed a treaty that agreed to use national currencies in bilateral trade and boost cross-currency settlements up to 50 percent (*Sputnik News, 2019; RT International, 2019b*). These

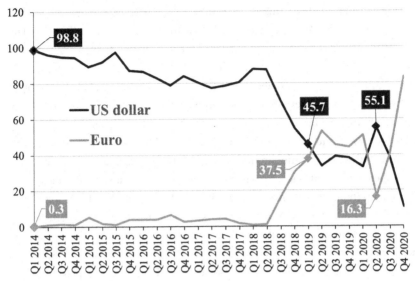

Figure 11 De-dollarization in Russia's exports to China (percent, Q1 2014–Q1 2021)

Source: Author compiled data from Bloomberg Financial and Bank of Russia.

developments suggest that Russia and China are moving closer to forming a de-dollarization hub as both of their relationships with the United States have deteriorated.

5.4 Disrupting the Dollar's Dominance in Global Equity Markets

The BRICS stock exchanges alliance is an interesting case of a BRICS coalition initiated by the market and mobilized through the market within the existing global financial system. This alliance idea was first suggested by the Hong Kong Exchanges and Clearing Limited (HKEx) in June 2010, shortly after South Africa joined the BRIC group (Taggart, 2011). In October 2011, stock exchanges in BRICS countries announced an initiative to cross-list benchmark equity index derivatives (*BW Businessworld, 2014*). This initiative brought together Brazil's BM&F BOVESPA, Russia's Moscow Interbank Currency Exchange from Russia, HKEx as the initial China representative, and South Africa's Johannesburg Stock Exchange. The National Stock Exchange of India (NSE) and the BSE Limited (formerly known as Bombay Stock Exchange) have signed letters of support and will join the alliance after finalizing outstanding requirements.

The BRICS leaders endorsed the formation of this equity market alliance at the 2012 BRICS Summit, and BRICS stock exchanges alliance also started cross-listing equity benchmark index derivatives that could be bought in local currencies during this summit.[19] Members of the BRICS stock exchanges alliance have planned three stages of implementation for the initiative. The first stage is the cross-listing of benchmark equity index derivatives, which is meant to facilitate liquidity growth in the BRICS markets and strengthen the international position of the BRICS alliance in the global economy.[20] Participating exchanges offer local currency-denominated benchmark equity index derivatives. In the second stage, members of the alliance plan to jointly develop new products for cross-listing on their exchanges. The third stage will include further cooperation in developing joint products and new services.

Although the BRICS stock exchanges alliance was not initiated with the goal of de-dollarization, the outcome is a step toward reducing the US dollar's dominance in global equities market. At the time of its announcement, the seven participating exchanges represented a combined listed market capitalization of USD9.02 trillion and an equity market trading value per month of USD422 billion, and 9,481 listed companies (Taggart, 2011). They also accounted for over 18 percent of all exchange-listed derivative contracts traded by volume worldwide at that time (Taggart, 2011). These exchanges collectively represent sizable and fast-growing equity markets that are not traded using the US dollar. Deeper cooperation through cross-listing and joint product development would facilitate the broader use of BRICS local currencies in these equity markets.

A BRICS exchanges alliance is appealing for investors in BRICS countries as well as those overseas. The alliance allows domestic investors within BRICS who want to go offshore to trade index futures and options for each exchange on their domestic market to use their own currency, which is free of capital controls or currency risk. For investors outside of the BRICS countries, the alliance offers easy access to major equity index derivatives of the BRICS markets, which gives them an opportunity for portfolio diversification and for gaining exposure to BRICS equity markets. Broader domestic and international participation in the cross-listed financial products will not only raise the profile of the exchanges but also increase the use of BRICS currencies in global equity markets and divert capital traffic away from the dollar-denominated financial assets. Moreover, for investors who already have exposure to BRICS

---

[19] The derivatives cross-listed includes Brazil's IBOVESPA futures, Russia's MICEX Index futures, India's Sensex index futures; Hong Kong's Hang Seng index futures and Hang Seng China Enterprises Index futures, and South Africa's FTSE/JSE Top 40 futures. For more details, see Daniel and Winter (2012); *The Economic Times* (2012), *Business Standard* (2013).

[20] The cross-listed derivatives include Brazil's IBOVESPA futures; Russia's MICEX Index futures; India's S&P BSE SENSEX Index futures; Hong Kong's Hang Seng Index futures and Hang Seng China Enterprises Index futures; and South Africa's FTSE/JSE Top40 futures. For more details, see Moscow Exchange (n.d.).

economies, futures are essential for hedging and risk management, which is a necessity for developing a robust financial ecosystem in BRICS countries.

To summarize the findings of this section, "reform-the-status-quo" initiatives have allowed BRICS members to reduce their dependence on the US dollar without creating new nondollar institutions or market mechanisms. These initiatives are less effective than "go-it-alone" measures due to the lack of nondollar alternatives. They are likely to be less successful in de-dollarizing the existing global financial system or enabling rising powers to achieve greater autonomy and influence in the global system. However, BRICS group-level initiatives, such as the launch of the CRA as a first line of defense before going to the IMF, and the collective bargaining for SDR reform, have demonstrated a high level of coalitional strength, as BRICS present a united front to the Western-dominated multilateral financial institutions. The sub-BRICS level de-dollarization initiatives, such as the unilateral reduction of the share of dollar assets in foreign exchange reserves and the BRICS stock exchanges alliance, directly improve members' autonomy. These measures, however, are of a much smaller scope.

Russia's aggressive reduction in its US dollar asset holdings suggests that for any country subject to US sanctions, its central bank and sovereign fund can unilaterally de-dollarize its reserve assets as one measure to attempt to weaken the effectiveness of US sanctions. However, in the context of BRICS, it is very unlikely that all BRICS central banks will agree to remove the dollar from their reserves. After all, the US dollar is still the most widely accepted currency in international settlements, and the US Treasury bond is still the best proxy for risk-free assets. The large dollar asset holdings of some BRICS members prevent them from dumping the US dollar or US Treasury securities on a large scale, as a decrease in US dollar asset value would inevitably incur major losses for these BRICS members. Moreover, the CRA has limited capacity to provide liquidity needs, and there is also a cap on withdrawals. This means the CRA can only serve as 'first line of defense' but not a 'lender of last resort' for the BRICS members. Finally, cross-listing among BRICS stock exchanges does not re-write the rules or standards of global capital markets. If these exchanges want to be attractive to international investors, they must establish regulatory certainty, with convertibility to the US dollar market. Moreover, compared with the dollar-based equity market, their size and market depth are much smaller. Therefore, at the current stage, BRICS stock exchanges have little capacity to create a large impact on global financial markets.

Finally, several of these reform measures require negotiations with the incumbent, such as the SDR reform. Collective actions involving only a small number of participants are much easier to mobilize than a multi-party negotiation, especially when the incumbent powers have significant control over the existing system. Even if there was an opportunity for a BRICS currency to be promoted and to share the dominant currency power position with the US dollar, there is no BRICS currency that could take this responsibility, the renminbi included. As long as the renminbi comes with the strings of capital controls attached, it cannot rise to the dominant currency position either in trade or international finance.

6 Conclusion and Implications for Future Research

This study has conceptualized coalitional de-dollarization and provided the first systematic analysis of the evolution of BRICS as a de-dollarization coalition. Using a risk management lens, it developed the "Pathways to De-dollarization" framework to explain how a rising power coalition can attempt to de-dollarize the US-led global financial system and mitigate the risk of dollar hegemony using both "go-it-alone" and "reform-the-status-quo" strategies and various institutional and market mechanisms.

Our framework contributes to existing scholarship on currency statecraft and global financial governance, the political economy of rising powers, and BRICS studies. Our conceptualization of coalitional de-dollarization has three primary theoretical implications. First, coalitional de-dollarization is different from national or unilateral monetary de-dollarization. Prior scholarship has demonstrated that national monetary de-dollarization is about the process of implementing domestic policies and regulations to institute a national currency at home. In contrast, coalitional de-dollarization revolves around international negotiation processes that require mutual gains to make the creation of nondollar multilateral institutions and an alternative nondollar infrastructure possible. While we initially hypothesized that Russia and countries most negatively affected by the dollar volatilities would emphasize "go-it-alone" strategies, we found growing support for de-dollarization and efforts to innovate in the de-dollarization space among all coalition members. We found that BRICS members do not have to prioritize de-dollarization for strategic reasons (e.g., avoiding sanctions) to use multiple de-dollarization pathways. Instead, their heterogeneous interests in the de-dollarization space allow them to jointly create value and "trade" across issues.

Second, our systematic examination of BRICS' coalitional de-dollarization initiatives speaks to the growing convergence among BRICS and the deepening of BRICS' economic cooperation despite the recent military conflict between India and China. The dynamic within BRICS demonstrates that de-dollarization is advocated by pivotal states – explicitly counter-hegemonic Russia and diversification-focused China that attempt to mobilize followers in order to create a broader nondollar-based sphere of influence. The challenge to the US dollar does not only come from US strategic adversaries or competitors but also from US allies and partners among BRICS who have economic incentives to reduce the dollar's dominance and hedge against exchange risk. Bypassing sanctions and geopolitical reasons prompt pivotal states to lead de-dollarization initiatives, but it is the shared economic incentives to reduce currency risk that sustain the de-dollarization coalition in the long term.

Third, our evaluation of de-dollarization initiatives takes place at different levels and demonstrates that unilateral de-dollarization initiatives could pave the way for a wider coalitional initiative. Connecting national nondollar financial infrastructures among BRICS can lead to the creation of an alternative nondollar financial system. Similarly, connecting BRICS-level initiatives with non-Western organizations' initiatives can generate benefits through institutional interactions.

Empirically, this study uses new BRICS cooperation data and BRICS de-dollarization as a case study, but it can also be applied to other aspiring de-dollarization coalitions. The findings are summarized in Figure 12. BRICS "go-it-alone" de-dollarization initiatives have taken place at all levels of coalitional strength. However, its "reform-the-status-quo" initiatives have thus far been mostly at the group, sub-group, and unilateral levels and have not yet made concrete achievements beyond the group level. BRICS has demonstrated a relatively high degree of coalitional strength in the pursuit of "go-it-alone" initiatives as evidenced in the use of the NDB for development finance de-dollarization; the members' commitment to a prospective BRICS alternative to SWIFT; its joint planning for a BRICS digital currency; and the broader BRICS Plus outreach efforts. Although these initiatives remain at a small scale, they create new nondollar mechanisms and help BRICS members achieve greater autonomy. Moreover, they also expand BRICS' influence by helping with the creation of a BRICS de-dollarization sphere of influence. Therefore, they provide critical components for developing an alternative nondollar financial system governed by BRICS.

Figure 13 visualizes the analyzed BRICS' de-dollarization initiatives against the key areas of the dollar's dominance. Our analysis finds that although Russia has been the most outspoken and the most active in pursuit of de-dollarization, China has the most capacity and presents the most credible challenge to the dollar hegemony among the BRICS members. Other members have been less enthusiastic toward de-dollarization, but they have nonetheless participated. That said, our original assumption that BRICS de-dollarization initiatives are

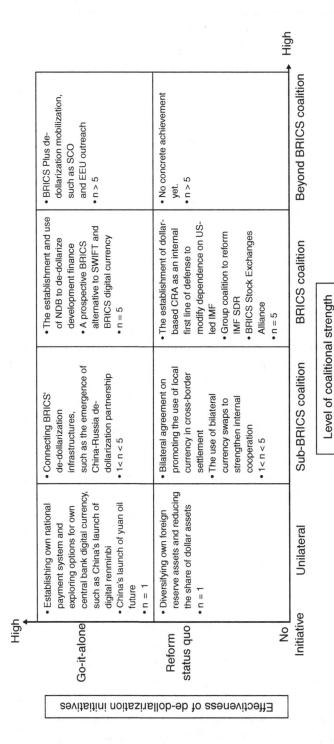

Figure 12 Evaluating BRICS as a de-dollarization coalition

Note: n = number of participants in a de-dollarization initiative (state actors and non-state actors). N = number of formal members in the rising power coalition (in the case of BRICS, N = 5, including Brazil, Russia, India, China, and South Africa).

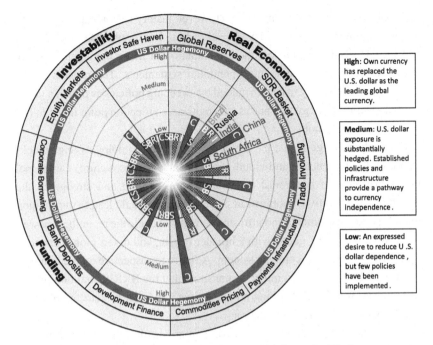

Figure 13 A visualization of BRICS progress along the "Pathways to De-dollarization"

not aiming at a wholesale throw-away of the dollar but rather a reaction against the dollar hegemony holds. We have illustrated the alternative financial infrastructure that enables BRICS members such as Russia to signal immunity to US sanctions and access global markets via a nondollar financial system. While Russia may be a unique strategic adversary, its behavior reminds one of former US Treasury Secretary Jack Lew's warning in 2016 that "the more we condition the use of the dollar and our financial system on adherence to US foreign policy, the more the risk of migration to other currencies and other financial systems in the medium-term grows" (Lew, 2016). We demonstrate that the risk of global finance migrating to an alternative financial system is real. While the immediate consequence of this shift is the decline in the US ability to use sanctions against its strategic adversaries such as Russia, the long-term challenges are immense, as sanction power is a critical tool that strengthens US leadership without the use of military force. Furthermore, it raises questions about US ability to advance its political and economic values in the global system and preserve a soft power edge.

To be sure, the US dollar is still the dominant currency in nearly every aspect of the current global financial system, and it is unlikely that another currency will replace the dollar any time soon. However, history reminds us that the US dollar's dominant status should not be assumed to last forever. De-dollarization is a secular trend that involves the accumulation of many incremental policy initiatives targeted at encouraging nondollar settlements. The process of de-dollarization is unlikely to be punctuated by sweeping policies as part of a grand de-dollarization strategy that marks a recognizable inflection point in the fall of the US dollar hegemony.

Our analysis suggests that the use of new financial technologies (e.g., block-chain, digital currencies, and cloud-based financial infrastructure) can propel the formation of a revisionist de-dollarization coalition and strengthen the credibility of collective mobilization. Such a coalition could lead to the creation of new market instruments and infrastructure that exclude the incumbent power, serve as global public goods with a broader buy-in, and divert global financial traffic away from the incumbent system. A future retrospective on the long-run process of de-dollarization might demonstrate that the BRICS coalition played a significant role in establishing an alternative nondollar system that precipitated broader global de-dollarization.

Our analysis suggests three promising areas for future research. First, we propose examining non-BRICS individual or coalitional contenders to the US dollar hegemony and how they interact with or complement BRICS. We addressed "BRICS Plus" mobilization, but greater attention must be paid to the dynamic of leader-follower relationships, particularly the Russia–China partnership in this space and the diffusion of their policies. Second, future research should explore how US allies (e.g., the EU) cooperate with US adversaries (e.g., Russia and Iran) on de-dollarization initiatives and related impacts on the United States. The EU has been developing alternatives to the dollar-based payment system and financial infrastructure. When the Trump administration reimposed sanctions on Iran in 2019, the EU not only developed its own mechanism to enable payments for Iranian oil but also partnered with Russia on cross-border payment infrastructure. Russia's removal of the US dollar in recent years has also led to its accumulation of euro reserves. Third, it is critical to study broader mobilization away from the US dollar that takes place in the digital space, considering the role of both state and non-state actors. We discussed BRICS Pay - a shared BRICS digital currency, BRICS alternatives to SWIFT - and individual BRICS' central bank digital currency development. However, the fintech sector is evolving rapidly, and it is linked to many other issue areas, such as cross-border payments, e-commerce, and financial security in cyberspace. Thus, examining the potential role of cryptocurrencies sponsored by private actors in de-dollarization is crucial. Certain BRICS members, such as China, are leading in this space and seek to become the new global agenda-setters and norm-makers. While this Element began to explore this challenge, further investigation of whether the United States can set global digital finance standards and maintain its global leadership in the digital era is an important direction for future research.

References

Abdenur, A. E., Folly, M., Moura, K., Jordão, S. A. S., and Maia, P. (2014). The BRICS and the South Atlantic: Emerging Arena for South–South Cooperation. *South African Journal of International Affairs*, vol. 21, no. 3, pp. 303–319.

ACRA Credit Rating. (2020, July 13). ACRA Affirms AAA to New Development Bank, Outlook Stable, under the International Scale and AAA(RU), Outlook Stable, under the National Scale for the Russian Federation. www.acra-ratings.com/press-releases/1949.

Aggarwal, P. (2020). On De-Risking and De-Dollarizing Intra-BRICS Trade via Smart Contracts. *BRICS Journal of Economics*, vol. 1, no. 4, pp. 54–69.

Aliaj, O., and Astrasheuskaya, N. (2019, October 24). Russia's Rosneft Switches All Export Contracts to Euros. *Financial Times*.

Amiti, S., and Mishra, R. (2014, May 30). Trade in Rupee. *Frontline*.

Andermo, E., and Kragh, M. (2021). Sanctions and Dollar Dependency in Russia: Resilience, Vulnerability, and Financial Integration. *Review of International Post Soviet Affairs*, vol. 37, no. 3, pp. 276–301.

Andrianova, A., and Doff, N. (2019, January 9). Russia Buys Quarter of World Yuan Reserves in Shift from Dollar. *Bloomberg*.

Antoniades, A. (2017). The New Resilience of Emerging and Developing Countries: Systemic Interlocking, Currency Swaps and Geoeconomics. *Global Policy*, vol. 8, no. 2, pp. 170–180.

Ayres, M., Mandl, C., and McGeever, J. (2020, November 16). Brazil Launches "Pix" Instant Payments System, Whatsapp to Enter "Soon." *Reuters*.

Bank for International Settlements. (2019). Triennial Central Bank Survey of Foreign Exchange and Over-the-Counter (OTC) Derivatives Markets in 2019. www.bis.org/statistics/derstats.htm.

Bank of Russia. (2020). A Digital Ruble: A Consultation Paper. www.cbr.ru/StaticHtml/File/113008/Consultation_Paper_201013_eng.pdf.

Banks am. (2019, January 3). BRICS is Creating a Common Payment System. https://banks.am/en/news/fintech/16946%20target=.

Belt and Road Initiative. (2021, March 25). 银联国际加快"一带一路"互联互通支付网络建设. http://ydyl.china.com.cn/2021-03-25/content_77344861.htm.

Biziwick, M., Cattaneo, N., and Fryer, D. (2015). The Rationale for and Potential Role of the BRICS Contingent Reserve Arrangement. *South African Journal of International Affairs*, vol. 22, no. 3, pp. 307–324.

Blinder, A. S. (1996). The Role of the Dollar as an International Currency. *Eastern Economic Journal*, vol. 22 (Spring), pp. 127–136.

Bloomberg News. (2021, April 18). China Says It Has No Desire to Replace Dollar with Digital Yuan. www.bloomberg.com/news/articles/2021-04-18/ china-to-focus-on-domestic-use-of-digital-fx-first-zhou-says

Brand South Africa. (2011, April 9). SA's BRICS Debut "Very Successful." www.brandsouthafrica.com/investments-immigration/business/19-apr-11-2811

Brazil MFA (Ministry of Foreign Affairs of Brazil). (2020, November 7). XII BRICS Summit Moscow Declaration. www.gov.br/mre/en/contact-us/press-area/press-releases/xii-brics-summit-moscow-declaration.

BRIC. (2009). Joint Statement of the BRIC Countries' Leaders. http://en.krem lin.ru/supplement/209.

BRICS. (2011). Sanya Declaration. https://mea.gov.in/bilateral-documents .htm?dtl/4789/Sanya+Declaration.

BRICS. (2013). BRICS and Africa: Partnership for Development, Integration and Industrialization. www.brics.utoronto.ca/docs/130327-statement.pdf.

BRICS. (2014). Treaty for the Establishment of a BRICS Contingent Reserve Arrangement. www.brics.utoronto.ca/docs/140715-treaty.html.

BRICS. (2016). Goa Declaration at 8th BRICS Summit. www.mea.gov.in/bilat eral-documents.htm?dtl/27491/Goa+Declaration+at+8th+BRICS+Summit.

BRICS. (2020). Strategy for BRICS Economic Partnership 2025. https://eng .brics-russia2020.ru/images/114/81/1148155.pdf.

BRICS-Russia. (2020). Road Map for BRICS Energy Cooperation up to 2025. https://brics-russia2020.ru/images/85/29/852976.pdf.

BRICS Business Council. (2020). 2020 BRICS Business Council Annual Report. https://brics-russia2020.ru/images/114/83/1148381.pdf.

BRICS India. (2021). Evolution of BRICS. https://brics2021.gov.in/about-brics.

Bruetsch, C., and Papa, M. (2013). Deconstructing the BRICS: Bargaining Coalition, Imagined Community or Geopolitical Fad? *Chinese Journal of International Politics*, vol. 6, no. 3, pp. 299–327.

Bryanski, G. (2009, June 16). Russia Calls for Revision of SDR Currency Basket. *Reuters*.

BtcoinAfrica. (2018, June 8). South African Central Bank Reports Successful Trial of Blockchain Project Khokha. https://bitcoinafrica.io/2018/06/08/ south-african-central-bank-project-khokha/

BusinessTech. (2021, March 4). The SARB is Looking at New Bank Cards for South Africa. https://businesstech.co.za/news/banking/472660/the-sarb-is-looking-at-new-bank-cards-for-south-africa/

BW Businessworld. (2014, November 8). BRICS Bourses Start Cross-Listing Derivative Indices. www.businessworld.in/article/BRICS-Bourses-Start-Cross-Listing-Derivative-Indices/08-11-2014-63533/

Carney, M. (2019, August 23). The Growing Challenges for Monetary Policy in the Current International Monetary and Financial System. Speech at the Jackson Hole Symposium 2019. www.bis.org/review/r190827b.pdf

Casas, C., Díez, F., Gopinath, G., and Gourinchas, P. O. (2017). Dollar Pricing Redux. Bank for International Settlements Working Papers No. 653. www .bis.org/publ/work653.pdf.

Catão, L., and Terrones, M. (2016). Financial De-Dollarization: A Global Perspective and the Peruvian Experience. IMF Working Papers No. 16 (97). https://papers.ssrn.com/sol3/papers.cfm?abstract_id=2882693

Central Bank of Brazil. (2020, June 18). Integrated Platform Using Blockchain for Licensing Financial Institutions Goes. www.bcb.gov.br/en/pressdetail/2337/nota.

Chaudhury, D. R. (2019a, April 20). Brazil Outlines Slew of Sectors for 2019 BRICS Summit under Its Presidency. *The Economic Times*.

Chaudhury, D. R. (2019b, November 14). India-Russia-China Explore Alternative to SWIFT Payment Mechanism. *The Economic Times*.

Chaudhury, D. R., and Pubby, M. (2019, August 30). Narendra Modi: Bilateral Trade in Rupee-Rouble Up 5-Fold during Modi Govt. *The Economic Times*.

Chengxin International Credit Rating. (2020). The New Development Bank Follow-up Credit Rating. www.chinamoney.com.cn/dqs/cm-s-notice-query/fileDownLoad.do?mode=open&contentId=1718952&priority=0

Chidley, C. (2014). Toward a Framework of Alignment in International Relations. *Politikon*, vol. 41, no. 1, pp. 141–157.

Chin, G. T. (2014). The BRICS-led Development Bank: Purpose and Politics Beyond the G20. *Global Policy*, vol. 5, no. 3, pp. 366–373.

China MOFA (Ministry of Foreign Affairs). (2015, July 10). Xi Jinping Attends Dialogue between Leaders of BRICS Countries, the EEU, the SCO Members and Observers and the Invited Countries. www.mfa.gov.cn/ce/cezm//eng/zgxw/t1280851.htm

China MOFA (Ministry of Foreign Affairs). (2017, June 19). Media Note of the Meeting of the BRICS Ministers of Foreign Affairs/International Relations. www.fmprc.gov.cn/mfa_eng/wjdt_665385/2649_665393/t1471323.shtml.

China MOFCOM (Ministry of Commerce). (2021). 俄媒称中俄本币结算七年增九倍. www.mofcom.gov.cn/article/i/jyjl/e/202101/20210103028115.shtml.

China News. (2016, September 14). 银联国际与俄罗斯国家支付卡公司首次开展发卡合作.

Chossudovsky, M. (2018, July 24). BRICS and the Fiction of "De-Dollarization." *Global Research*.

CIPS World Service. (2020a). CIPS Traffic by Month. www.cips.com.cn/cip sen/index.html.

CIPS World Service. (2020b). CIPIS Introduction. www.cips.com.cn/cips/_2664/_2708/33604/index.html.

Cohen, B. J. (2002). US Policy on Dollarisation: A Political Analysis. *Geopolitics*, vol. 7 (Summer), pp. 5–26.

Cohen, B. J. (2005a). The Macrofoundation of Monetary Power. EUI Working Paper RSCAS No. 2005/08. http://hdl.handle.net/1814/3357.

Cohen, B. J. (2015b). *Currency Power: Understanding Monetary Rivalry*. Princeton: Princeton University Press

Cohen, B. J. (2018). *Currency Statecraft: Monetary Rivalry and Geopolitical Ambition*. Chicago: University of Chicago Press.

Cohen, B. J, Kirshner, J., and Helleiner, E. (2014). *The Great Wall of Money: Power and Politics in China's International Monetary Relations*. Ithaca: Cornell University Press

Cooper, A. F. (2017). The BRICS' New Development Bank: Shifting from Material Leverage to Innovative Capacity. *Global Policy*, vol. 8, no. 3, pp. 275–278.

Cooper, A. F., and Farooq, A. B. (2013). BRICS and the Privileging of Informality in Global Governance. *Global Policy*, vol. 4, no. 4, pp. 428–433.

Dai, X. (1999, September). *Statement by Mr. Dai Xianglong Governor, People's Bank of China*, Fifty-Third Meeting of the Interim Committee of the Board of Governors of the International Monetary System. Full speech transcript is available at www.imf.org/external/am/1999/icstate/chn.htm.

Danese, P. (August 24, 2016). RMB on the rise in South Africa, says Swift. *Global Capital*. www.globalcapital.com/asia/article/28mykgkc1iui598rg 191c/china/rmb-on-the-rise-in-south-africa-says-swift

Daniel, F. J., and Winter, B. (2012, March 28). UPDATE 1-BRICS to Eye Joint Bank, Stock Exchange Tie-up at Summit. *Reuters*.

Dash, P., Sharma, M., and Nizami, G., (2019). Trade in Local Currency: Illustration of India's Rupee Trade with Nepal, Iran and Russia. *Research and Information System for Developing Countries Discussion Paper* No.237.

Didier, L. (2017). South-South Trade and Geographical Diversification of Intra-SSA Trade: Evidence from BRICs: South-South Trade. *African Development Review*, vol. 29, no. 2, pp. 39–154.

Diko, N., and Sempijja, N. (2021a). Conduit for Economic Growth and Development? Exploring South Africa and Brazil's BRICS Membership. *Politikon*, vol. 48, no. 3, pp. 355-371.

Diko, N., and Sempijja, N. (2021b). Does Participation in BRICS Foster South-South cooperation? Brazil, South Africa, and the Global South. *Journal of Contemporary African Studies*, vol. 39, no. 1, pp. 151–167.

Dilasha, S. (October 8, 2013). Curbing Volatility: India, South Africa Plan to Settle Trade in Local Currencies. *The Economic Times*. https://economic times.indiatimes.com/news/economy/foreign-trade/curbing-volatility-india-south-africa-plan-to-settle-trade-in-local-currencies/articleshow/23675225 .cms

Doman-b. (June 16, 2009). Expand SDR Basket to Include Yuan, Gold: Russia News. *Doman-b.com* www.domain-b.com/organisation/imf/20090616_dmi try_medvedev.html

Drezner, D. W. (2019). Counter-Hegemonic Strategies in the Global Economy. *Security Studies*, vol. 28, no.3, pp. 505–531.

Drezner, D., Farrell, H., and Newman, A. (Eds.). (2021). *The Uses and Abuses of Weaponized Interdependence*. Washington, DC: Brookings Institution Press.

Du, J. (2015, June 4). Yuan to be used for Sino-Russia Oil Trade. *China Daily*.

Deutsche Welle. (2018, November 9). Russia and China to Reduce Use of US Dollar in Trade. *Deutsche Welle*.

Economic Times. (2009, June 15). India Reluctant to Join De-dollarization Chorus at BRIC. https://economictimes.indiatimes.com/news/economy/pol icy/india-reluctant-to-join-de-dollarisation-chorus-at-bric/articleshow/ 4659464.cms

Economic Times. (2012a, March 15). BRICS SEs to Cross-list Index Derivatives. https://economictimes.indiatimes.com/brics-ses-to-cross-list-index-derivatives/articleshow/12270658.cms

Business Standard. (2013, January 21). BRICS Bourses to Cross-list Benchmark Equity Index Derivatives. www.business-standard.com/article/ markets/brics-bourses-to-cross-list-benchmark-equity-index-derivatives-112031400202_1.html

Economic Times. (2013, October 6). BRICS can Set Up Mechanism for Trade in Local Currency: Rob Davies. https://economictimes.indiatimes.com/ news/economy/foreign-trade/brics-can-set-up-mechanism-for-trade-in-local-currency-rob-davies/articleshow/23603582.cms

Eichengreen, B. (2012). *Exorbitant Privilege: The Rise and Fall of the Dollar and the Future of the International Monetary System*. Oxford: Oxford University Press.

Eichengreen, B., and Flandreau, Marc (2008). *The Rise and Fall of the Dollar, or when did the Dollar Replace Sterling as the Leading International Currency?* Cambridge: National Bureau of Economic Research.

EIU ViewsWire. (2016, June 24). South Africa Economy: The Impact of China's Slowdown on South Africa. *Economist Intelligence Unit ViewsWire*.

Ekberg, J., and Ho, M. (2021). *A New Dawn for Digital Currency: Why China's eCNY Will Change the Way Money Flows Forever*. Oliver Wyman. www .oliverwyman.com/content/dam/oliver-wyman/v2/publications/2021/may/ a-new-dawn-for-digital-currency.pdf

Electronic Payments International. (2020, December 29). UnionPay to Accelerate Contactless Payments in Russia with Solidarnost Bank, Huawei. Retrieved July 9, 2021, from www.electronicpaymentsinternational.com/ news/unionpay-to-accelerate-contactless-payments-in-russia-with-solidar nost-bank-huawei/.

Escobar, P. (2019, August 29). BRICS was Created as a Tool of Attack: Lula. *Asia Times*. https://asiatimes.com/2019/08/brics-was-created-as-a-tool-of-attack-lula/

Farchy, J. (2015, June 1). Gazprom Neft Sells Oil to China in Renminbi rather than Dollars. *Financial Times*. www.ft.com/content/8e88d464-0870-11e5-85de-00144feabdc0

Farrell, H., and Newman, A. (2019). Weaponized Interdependence: How Global Economic Networks Shape State Coercion. *International Security*, vol. 44, no. 1, pp. 42–79.

Financial Tribune. (2019, September 17). Banks in Iran, Russia Connected via Non-SWIFT Financial Messaging Service. https://financialtribune.com/art icles/business-and-markets/99912/banks-in-iran-russia-connected-via-non-swift-financial-messaging

Fitch Ratings. (2019, December 3). Fitch Assigns New Development Bank's Euro Medium-Term Notes Programme "AA+" Rating. www.fitchratings .com/research/banks/fitch-assigns-new-development-bank-euro-medium-term-notes-programme-aa-exp-rating-03-12-2019

Flemes, D. (2009). India-Brazil-South Africa (IBSA) in the New Global Order. *International Studies*, vol. 46, no. 4, pp. 401–421.

Foster, J. (2018). *Oil and World Politics: The Real Story of Today's Conflict Zones: Iraq, Afghanistan, Venezuela, Ukraine and More*. Toronto: James Lorimer.

Friedman, T. L. (1991, July 11). Bush Lifts a Ban on Economic Ties to South Africa. *The New York Times*.

Gajara, D. (2020, February 29). India among Most Dollarised Countries in Terms of Invoicing. *The Hindu*.

Gallagher, K. P. (2015). Contesting the Governance of Capital Flows at the IMF. *Governance*, vol. 28, no. 2), pp. 185–198.

Ghosh, S. (2021, February 24). India's Central Bank Voices "Major Concerns" About Crypto. *Bloomberg*.

Goddard, S. E. (2018). Embedded Revisionism: Networks, Institutions, and Challenges to World Order. *International Organization*, vol. 72, no. 4, pp. 763–797.

Goldberg, L. (2011). The International Role of the Dollar: Does It Matter if This Changes? Staff Report, No. 522, New York: Federal Reserve Bank of New York.

Gopinath, G., Boz, E., Casas, C., Díez, F. J., Gourinchas, P. O., and Plagborg-Møller, M. (2020). Dominant Currency Paradigm. *American Economic Review*, vol. 110, no. 3, pp. 677-719.

Gopinath, G., and Stein, J. C., (2021). Banking, Trade, and the Making of a Dominant Currency. *The Quarterly Journal of Economics*, vol. 136, no. 2, pp. 783–830.

Gopinath, G., and Zwaanstra, J. (2017, December 21). Dollar Dominance in Trade: Facts and Implications. *India Exim Bank*. www.eximbankindia.in/blog/blog-content.aspx?BlogID=9&BlogTitle=Dollar%20Dominance%20in%20Trade:%20Facts%20and%20Implications

Groepe, F. (2018, June). *Opening Remarks by Francois Groepe, Deputy Governor of the South African Reserve Bank, at the launch of the Project Khokha Report*. Johannesburg: Sandton Convention Centre www.bis.org/review/r180607e.pdf.

Gruber, L. (2000). *Ruling the World: Power Politics and the Rise of Supranational Institutions*. Princeton: Princeton University Press.

Haig, S. (2020, February 20). Brazilian Central Bank Promises Instant Payment Platform to Compete With Crypto. *Cointelegraph*.

Hamilton, A. (2019, November 20). BRICS Nations Aiming for Common Payment System. *FinTech Futures*.

Han, Z., and Paul, T. V. (2020). China's Rise and Balance of Power Politics. *The Chinese Journal of International Politics*, vol. 13, no. 1, pp. 1–26.

Hancock, T. (2019, August 6). 'Brics Bank' Seeks Move Away from Dollar Funding. *Financial Times*.

Helleiner, E., and Kirshner, J. (2009). *The Future of the Dollar*. Ithaca: Cornell University Press.

Helleiner, E., and Wang, H. (2018). Limits to the BRICS' Challenge: Credit Rating Reform and Institutional Innovation in Global Finance. *Review of International Political Economy*, vol. 25, no.5, pp. 573–595.

Henning, C. R. (2017). *Tangled Governance: International Regime Complexity, the Troika, and the Euro Crisis*. Oxford: Oxford University Press, p. 23.

Hirschman, A. O. (1970). *Exit, Voice, and Loyalty: Responses to Decline in Firms, Organizations, and States*. Cambridge, MA: Harvard University Press.

Hillman, J. (2020). China and Russia: Economic Unequals. Center for Strategic & International Studies Report.

Hindu Business Line. (2019, August 22). BRICS Bank Looks to Tap into Indian Rupee Offshore Market. www.thehindubusinessline.com/markets/forex/brics-bank-looks-to-tap-into-indian-rupee-offshore-market/article29224243.ece

Hopewell, K. (2017). The BRICS – Merely a Fable? Emerging Power Alliances in Global Trade Governance. *International Affairs*, vol. 93, no. 6, pp. 1377–1396.

Huotari, M., and Hanemann, T. (2014). Emerging Powers and Change in the Global Financial Order, *Global Policy*, vol. 5, no. 3, pp. 298–310.

Ikenberry, J., and Nexon, D. (2019). Hegemony Studies 3.0: The Dynamics of Hegemonic Orders. *Security Studies*, vol. 28, no. 3, pp. 395–421.

Invesforesight. (2018, October 4). PM will Urgently Approve Dedollarization Plan. https://investforesight.com/pm-will-urgently-approve-dedollarization-plan/.

Intergovernmental Fintech Working Group. (2021, February 11). *Press Release on the Intergovernmental Fintech Working Group (IFWG) launch of Project Khokha 2*, Intergovernmental Fintech Working Group of South Africa. www.ifwg.co.za/wp-content/uploads/PK2_IFWG_PressRelease_Project_Launch.pdf

Japan Credit Rating Agency. (2019). JCR Issuer Report: The New Development Bank. www.jcr.co.jp/en/ratinglist/sovereign/11009#

Japan Credit Rating Agency. (2020). JCR Issuer Report: The New Development Bank. www.jcr.co.jp/en/ratinglist/sovereign/11009#

Jupille, J., Mattli, W., and Snidal, D. (2013) *Institutional Choice and Global Commerce*. Cambridge: Cambridge University Press.

Kahler, M. (2013). Rising Powers and Global Governance: Negotiating Change in a Resilient Status Quo. *International Affairs*, vol. 89, no. (3), pp. 711–729.

Kamath, K. V. (2020). *Speech of Mr. K. V. Kamath, President, New Development Bank at the Fifth Annual Meeting of the Board of Governors.* Fifth Annual Meeting of the Board of Governors. www.ndb.int/president_desk/speech-mr-k-v-kamath-president-new-development-bank-fifth-annual-meeting-board-governors/

Kantchev, G. (2021, June 3). Russia's Wealth Fund to Ditch Dollar Amid US Sanctions Threat. *Wall Street Journal.* www.wsj.com/articles/russias-wealth-fund-to-ditch-dollar-amid-u-s-sanctions-threat-11622730123

Katada, S. N., Roberts, C., and Armijo, L. E. (2017). The Varieties of Collective Financial Statecraft: The BRICS and China, *Political Science Quarterly*, vol. 132, no. 3, pp. 403–433.

Kelly, B. (2009, June 28). Brazil, Russia, India, and China (the BRICs) Throw Down the Gauntlet on Monetary System Reform. *East Asia Forum*.

Khadbai, B. (2020, June 18). NDB Eyes Euros, Sterling and Triple-A Status. *Global Capital*.

Kievich, A. V. (2018). De–dollarization of the World Economy as an Objective Reality. https://core.ac.uk/download/pdf/214860318.pdf.

Kirshner, J. (1995) *Currency and Coercion: The Political Economy of International Monetary Power*. Princeton: Princeton University Press

Kirshner, J. (2008). Dollar Primacy and American Power: What's at Stake?. *Review of International Political Economy*, vol.15, no. 3, pp. 418–438.

Kirton, J., and Larionova, M. (Eds.). (2018). *BRICS and Global Governance*. New York: Routledge.

Kring, W. N., and Gallagher, K. P. (2019). Strengthening the Foundations? Alternative Institutions for Finance and Development. *Development and Change*, vol. 50, issue 1, pp. 3–23.

Kruck, A., and Zangl, B. (2020). The Adjustment of International Institutions to Global Power Shifts: A Framework for Analysis. *Glob Policy*, 11: 5-16

Labetskaya, K. (2012, May 23). Sergei Ryabkov: "BRICS is a Catalyst for Global Governance Reform." *Russia Beyond*. www.rbth.com/articles/2012/05/23/sergei_ryabkov_brics_is_a_catalyst_for_global_governance_reform_15691.html

Ladasic, I. K. (2017). De-dollarization Of Oil And Gas Trade. *17th International Multidisciplinary Scientific GeoConference SGEM 2017*, no.15, pp. 99–106.

Lauria, V., and Fumagalli, C. (2019). BRICS, the Southern Model, and the Evolving Landscape of Development Assistance: Toward a New Taxonomy. *Public Administration and Development*, vol. 39, no. 4–5, pp. 215–230.

Leahy, J. (2015, September 9). S&P cuts Brazil's Credit Rating to Junk. *Financial Times*.

Lew, J. (2016, March 30). Remarks of Secretary Lew on the Evolution of Sanctions and Lessons for the Future at the Carnegie Endowment for International Peace, U.S Department of Treasury. www.treasury.gov/press-center/press-releases/Pages/jl0398.aspx.

Li, L. (2019). BRICS: A Limited Role in Transforming the World. *Strategic Analysis*, vol. 43, no. 6, pp. 499–508.

Lianhe Credit Rating (2016). Credit Rating for NDB in 2016. www.lhratings.com/reports/A003174-XMZQ06618-2016.pdf.

Lipscy, P. Y. (2015). Explaining Institutional Change: Policy Areas, Outside Options, and the Bretton Woods Institutions. *American Journal of Political Science*, vol. 59, no. 2, pp. 341–356.

Lipton, M. (2017). Are the BRICS Reformers, Revolutionaries, or Counter-Revolutionaries? *South African Journal of International Affairs*, vol. 24, no.1, pp. 41–59.

Liu, C. (2016, December 18). UnionPay Cards Expanding Globally. *China Daily*.

Liu, X. (2014). Reflection upon China's Participation in the Remaking of Global Financial System (中国参与国际货币体系重塑的思考). *China Development Observation* (中国发展观察), vol. 12, pp.12–14.

Lopes, M., and Flak, A. (2013, March 26). China, Brazil Sign Trade, Currency Deal before BRICS Summit. *Reuters*.

Luckhurst, J. (2013). Building Cooperation between the BRICS and Leading Industrialized States. *Latin American Policy*, vol. 4, no. 2, pp. 251–268.

Luft, G. (2018, August 27). The Anti-dollar Awakening could be Ruder and Sooner than most Economists Predict. www.cnbc.com/2018/08/27/the-anti-dollar-awakening-could-be-ruder-and-sooner-than-most-economists-predict.html.

Mahrenbach, L. C. (2019). Conceptualising Emerging Powers, in T. M. Shaw, L. C. Mahrenbach, R. Modi and Y. C. Xu, (eds.), *The Palgrave Handbook of Contemporary International Political Economy*, Basingstoke: Palgrave Macmillan UK, pp. 217–232.

Maryam, J., Banday, U. J., and Mittal, A. (2018). Trade Intensity and Revealed Comparative Advantage: An Analysis of Intra-BRICS Trade. *International Journal of Emerging Markets*, vol. 13, no. 5, pp. 1182–1195.

Maasdorp, L. (2019). BRICS' New Development Bank Turns Four: What has it Achieved? World Economic Forum. www.weforum.org/agenda/2019/09/brics-new-development-bank-four-sustainability/

Macias, A., and Turak, N. (2021, April 15). Biden Administration Slaps New Sanctions on Russia for Cyberattacks, Election Interference. www.cnbc.com/2021/04/15/biden-administration-sanctions-russia-for-cyber-attacks-election-interference.html.

Mathews, J. A., and Selden, M. (2018). China: The Emergence of the Petroyuan and the Challenge to US Dollar Hegemony. *Asia-Pacific Journal: Japan Focus*, vol. 16, no. 22, p. 3.

McDowell, D. (2019). The (Ineffective) Financial Statecraft of China's Bilateral Swap Agreements. *Development and Change*, vol. 50, no. 1, pp. 122–143.

McDowell, D. (2020). Financial Sanctions and Political Risk in the International Currency System. *Review of International Political Economy*, vol. 28, no. 3, pp. 635–661.

Medvedev, D. (2019). Speech during the first BRIC Group Summit in Yekaterinburg. http://en.kremlin.ru/events/president/transcripts/4475

MercoPress. (2009, June 30). Brazil-China Bilateral Trade in Real and Yuan instead of US Dollar.Moscow Exchange. (n.d.). BRICS Exchanges Alliance. www.moex.com/s506

Moscow Times. (2019a, September 9). Russia's Massive Gold Stash Is Now Worth More Than $100Bln. www.themoscowtimes.com/2019/09/09/russias-massive-gold-stash-is-now-worth-more-than-100bln-a67202

Moscow Times. (2019b, November 14). Russia Says BRICS Nations Favor Idea of Common Payment System. www.themoscowtimes.com/2019/11/14/putin-to-invite-china-and-india-to-join-anti-sanctions-bank-network-a68172

Nelson, D. (2020, September 4). Brazil's Central Bank Says Nation Might Be Ready for a Digital Currency by 2022. *CoinDesk*. www.coindesk.com/markets/2020/09/03/brazils-central-bank-says-nation-might-be-ready-for-a-digital-currency-by-2022/

Nelson, D. (2021, February 12). Ex-CFTC Chair Christopher Giancarlo Stumps for Digital Dollar. *CoinDesk*. www.coindesk.com/policy/2021/02/12/ex-cftc-chair-christopher-giancarlo-stumps-for-digital-dollar/

New Development Bank (NDB). (2017). *NDB's General Strategy:2017-2021*. New Development Bank. www.ndb.int/wp-content/uploads/2017/07/NDB-Strategy-Final.pdf

NDB. (2014, July 15). *Agreement on the New Development Bank*. New Development Bank. www.ndb.int/wp-content/themes/ndb/pdf/Agreement-on-the-New-Development-Bank.pdf

NDB. (2019). *Annual Report 2019*. www.ndb.int/annual-report-2019/

NDB. (2019, November 25). NDB Registers RUB 100 billion bond programme in Russia. www.ndb.int/press_release/ndb-registers-rub-100-billion-bond-programme-russia/

NDB. (2021, March 25). NDB issues RMB 5 billion Sustainable Development Goals Bond. www.ndb.int/press_release/ndb-issues-rmb-5-billion-sustainable-development-goals-bond/

Nikolskaya, P. (2017, August 7). Moscow to cut dependence on US payment systems: RIA. *Reuters*.

Nogueira Batista Jr., P. (2019). *O Brasil Não Cabe No Quintal De Ninguém* (Brazil Does Not Fit in Anybody's Yard). Casa da Palavra/LeYa.

Nuruzzaman, M. (2020). Why BRICS Is No Threat to the Post-war Liberal World Order, *International Studies*, vol. 57, no.1, pp. 51–66.

Osborn, G. T.-F., Andrew. (2021, March 22). Russia's Top Diplomat Starts China Visit with Call to Reduce US Dollar Use. *Reuters*.

Overholt, W. H. (2016). *Renminbi rising: A New Global Monetary System Emerges*. Chichester, West Sussex, United Kingdom: John Wiley & Sons.

Pacheco, F. (2016, February 17). Brazil's Rating Cut Further into Junk Territory by S&P – Bloomberg. *Bloomberg*. www.bloomberg.com/news/articles/2016-02-17/brazil-s-credit-rating-cut-further-into-junk-territory-by-s-p

Palmer, D. (2019, November 15). BRICS Nations Ponder Digital Currency to Ease Trade, Reduce USD Reliance. *CoinDesk*.

Pandit, P. (2019). Delivering "Public Goods" and the Changing Financial Architecture: can BRICS Meet Expectations? *Third World Thematics: A TWQ Journal*, vol. 4, no. 6, pp. 475–488.

Pape, R. A. (2005). Soft Balancing Against the United States. *International Security*, vol. 30, no. 1, pp. 7–45.

Parmar, B. (2018, January 24). National Payments Corp gets nod to tie up with China UnionPay. *The Hindu Business Line*.

Partz, H. (2020, October 16). Five Russian Banks Express Interest in Piloting Digital Ruble. *Cointelegraph*.

People's Bank of China. (2016, January 20). 人民银行：进一步明确数字货币战略目标. www.gov.cn/xinwen/2016-01/20/content_5034826.htm.

People's Daily. (2017, September 5). Chair's Statement of the Dialogue of Emerging Market and Developing Countries. *People's Daily Online*. http://en.people.cn/n3/2017/0905/c90000-9264684.html

People's Daily. (2019, October 11). "银联国际与俄银行联手在莫斯科地铁开通手机闪付," *People's Daily Online*. http://world.people.com.cn/n1/2019/1011/c1002-31395157.html

Pine Labs. (2018, December 12). UnionPay International Debit & Credit Card Payment: Pine Labs Partner to expand visibility in India. www.pinelabs.com/media-analyst/unionpay-international-partners-with-pine-labs-to-expand-visibility-in-india.

Portes, R., and Rey, H. (1998). The Emergence of the Euro as an International Currency, in D. Begg, J. von Hagen, C. Wyplosz, and K. F. Zimmermann (eds.), *EMU: Prospects and Challenges for the Euro*, Oxford: Blackwell, pp. 307–304.

Prasad, E. (2016). *Gaining Currency: The Rise of the Renminbi*. New York: Oxford University Press.

PRC Gov. (The People's Republic of China offical government website). (2017, October 12). 我国外汇市场建立人民币对外币同步交收机制; 有利于消除本金交割风险, 防范交收时差风险, www.gov.cn. www.gov.cn/xinwen/2017-10/12/content_5231192.htm.

PRC Gov. (2019, June 6). 中俄元首签署《中华人民共和国和俄罗斯联邦关于发展新时代全面战略协作伙伴关系的联合声明. Retrieved July 9, 2021, from www.gov.cn/xinwen/2019-06/06/content_5397860.htm.

Putin, V. (2017, September 1). BRICS: Toward New Horizons of Strategic Partnership. http://en.kremlin.ru/events/president/news/55487.

Qobo, M., and Soko, M. (2015). The Rise of Emerging Powers in the Global Development Finance Architecture: The Case of the BRICS and the New Development Bank. *South African Journal of International Affairs*, vol. 22, no. 3, pp. 277–288.

Que, C., and Li, D. (2014). Global Economic Imbalance and the Reform of Global Currency System (全球经济失衡与国际货币体系改革). *Research on Financial and Economic Issues* (财经问题研究), vol. 2, pp. 37-45.

Quinna, S., and Roberds, W. (2016). Death of a Reserve Currency. *International Journal of Central Banking*. vol.12, no. 4, pp. 63–103.

Radulescu, I. G., Panait, M., and Voica, C. (2014). BRICS Countries Challenge to the World Economy New Trends. *Procedia Economics and Finance*, vol. 8, pp. 605–613.

RBC. (2019, November 14). "В БРИКС предложили создать единую криптовалюту для альянса," (BRICS proposed to create a single crypto-currency for the alliance). www.rbc.ru/economics/14/11/2019/5dcd27a 49a794738b8c6fdd8

Ray, R., and Simmons, B. A. (2020). *Tracking China's Overseas Development Finance*. Global Development Policy Center, Boston: Boston University.

Reserve Bank of India. (2018, April 5). Statement on Developmental and Regulatory Policies. www.rbi.org.in/Scripts/BS_PressReleaseDisplay.aspx? prid=43574

Reuters. (2014, October 13). China, Russia Sign $25 Billion Local Currency Swap. www.reuters.com/article/us-china-economy-forex/china-russia-sign-25-billion-local-currency-swap-idUSKCN0I20US20141013

Reuters. (2015, April 10). South Africa Signs $4.8 bln Currency Swap with China. www.reuters.com/article/ozabs-us-safrica-cenbank-idAFKBN0 N10RO20150410

Reuters. (2018, January 11). S&P cuts Brazil Credit Rating as Pension Reform Doubts Grow. www.reuters.com/article/brazil-sovereign-downgrade/sp-cuts-brazil-credit-rating-as-pension-reform-doubts-grow-idUSL1N1P628Y

Reuters. (2019a, March 19). Russia Backs Global Use of its Alternative SWIFT System. www.reuters.com/article/russia-banks-swift/russia-backs-global-use-of-its-alternative-swift-system-idUSL8N2163BU

Reuters. (2019b, October 8). Russia, Turkey Agree on Using Ruble, Lira in Mutual Settlements. www.reuters.com/article/russia-turkey-forex/russia-tur key-agree-on-using-rouble-lira-in-mutual-settlements-idUSR4N26O04T

Reuters. (2019c, November 14). Russia Says BRICS Nations Favor Idea of Common Payment System. www.reuters.com/article/uk-brics-summit-rus

sia-fx/russia-says-brics-nations-favour-idea-of-common-payment-system-idUSKBN1XO1KQ

Reuters. (2020, July 30). FACTBOX-China's Onshore Yuan Clearing and Settlement System CIPS. www.reuters.com/article/china-banks-clearing/fact box-chinas-onshore-yuan-clearing-and-settlement-system-cips-idUSL3N 2F115E

Roberts, C. A, Armijo, L. Elliott, and Katada, S. N. (2017). *The BRICS and Collective Financial Statecraft*. New York: Oxford University Press.

Rolfe, A. (2018, November 28). China and Russia to Launch New Payments System to Avoid the US Dollar. *Payments Cards & Mobile*. www.pay mentscardsandmobile.com/china-and-russia-to-launch-new-payments-system/

RT. (2014, July 15). BRICS Establish $100bn Bank and Currency Pool to Cut Out Western Dominance. www.rt.com/business/173008-brics-bank-cur rency-pool/

RT International. (2017, September 4). BRICS Countries Considering Own Cryptocurrency as Settlement Mechanism. www.rt.com/business/401969-brics-consider-joint-cryptocurrency/

RT International. (2018, October 2). Putin Backs Plan to De-dollarize Russian Economy. www.rt.com/business/440095-putin-russian-economy-dedollarisation/

RT International. (2019a, June 5). Dollar Dump? Russia & China Agree to Bilateral Trade in National Currencies during Putin-Xi Meeting. www.rt .com/business/461147-russia-china-nuclear-reactors/

RT International. (2019b, June 28). Russia & China Agree to Significantly Boost Trade in Ruble and Yuan at the Expense of the US Dollar. www.rt .com/business/462884-russia-china-ruble-yuan-trade/

Russia – Credit Rating. (n.d.). Retrieved July 8, 2021, from https://tradingeco nomics.com/russia/rating.

Russia Briefing. (2019, October 3). Russia's SPFS Alternative Payment Network Enters International Markets. www.russia-briefing.com/news/rus sias-spfs-alternative-payment-network-enters-international-markets.html/.

Russian Matters. (2018, July). Claim in 2018: "Russia relies heavily on energy exports for close to three-quarters of its export earnings and over half of its budget". Russian Matters, Belfer Center for Science and International Affairs, Harvard Kennedy School. www.russiamatters.org/node/11300.

Russia Business Today. (2019, October 28). Russia to Use SWIFT Alternative in Trade with China, India: Report. https://russiabusinesstoday.com/econ omy/russia-to-use-swift-alternative-in-trade-with-china-india-report/

Schoeman, M. (2015). South Africa as an Emerging Power: From Label to "Status Consistency"? *South African Journal of International Affairs*, vol. 22, no. 4, pp. 429–445.

Shanghai Cooperation Organization. (2006, June 15). Joint Communiqué of The Meeting of the Council of Heads of State of the Shanghai Cooperation Organization, China Internet Information Center. www.china.org.cn/english/features/meeting/171590.htm.

Shchedrov, O. (2009, March 31). Medvedev Urges Discussion on New Currency System. *Reuters*. www.reuters.com/article/uk-g20-russia-currencies-sb/medvedev-urges-discussion-on-new-currency-system-idUKTRE52U6FA20090331

Shead, S. (2021, June 3). Russia says it will remove dollar assets from its wealth fund. *CNBC*. www.cnbc.com/2021/06/03/russia-to-remove-dollar-assets-from-national-wealth-fund.html

Shome, A. (2021, March 11). Bank of Russia Plans to Pilot Digital Ruble in 2021 End. *Finance Magnates*. www.financemagnates.com/cryptocurrency/news/bank-of-russia-plans-to-pilot-digital-ruble-in-2021-end/

Simes, D. (2020, August 6). China and Russia ditch dollar in move toward "financial alliance." *Nikkei Asia*. https://asia.nikkei.com/Politics/International-relations/China-and-Russia-ditch-dollar-in-move-toward-financial-alliance

Singh, S. P., and Dube, M. (2014). BRICS and World Order: A Beginner's Guide. SSRN: https://ssrn.com/abstract=2443652.

Soldatkin, V. (2016, November 4). Russia Eyes Unified Payment Systems with China: PM. *Reuters*. www.reuters.com/article/us-russia-china-payments-sanctions/russia-eyes-unified-payment-systems-with-china-pm-idUSKBN12Z1RU

South Africa – Credit Rating. (2021). Retrieved July 8, 2021, from https://tradingeconomics.com/south-africa/rating.

South African Reserve Bank. (2018, June 5). South African Reserve Bank Releases Project Khokha Report, South African Government. www.gov.za/speeches/south-african-reserve-bank-releases-project-khokha-report-5-jun-2018-0000.

Sputnik News. (2019, June 28). Russia, China Sign Agreement on Payments in National Currencies in Blow to Dollar – Reports. https://sputniknews.com/20190628/russia-china-national-currencies-agreement-1076081592.html

Srivats, K. R. (2018, August 10). Blockchain: Exim Bank signs MoU with BRICS development banks. *The Hindu Business Line*. www.thehindubusinessline.com/money-and-banking/blockchain-exim-bank-signs-mou-with-brics-development-banks/article24655306.ece

Stella, P., and Lönnberg, Å. (2008). Issues in Central Bank Finance and Independence. IMF Working Paper WP/08/37.

Stephen, M. D., and Parízek, M. (2019). New Powers and the Distribution of Preferences in Global Trade Governance: From Deadlock and Drift to Fragmentation. *New Political Economy*, vol. 24, no. 6, pp. 735–758.

Snyder, G. H. (1997). *Alliance Politics*. Ithaca, NY: Cornell University Press.

Steiner, A. (2014). Current Account Balance and Dollar Standard: Exploring the Linkages. *Journal of International Money and Finance*, vol. 41, pp. 65–94.

Stuenkel, O. (2014). Emerging Powers and Status: The Case of the First BRICs Summit. *Asian Perspective*, vol. 38, no. 1, pp. 89–109.

Subacchi, P. (2016). *The People's Money: How China is Building a Global Currency*. La Vergne: Columbia University Press.

Suchodolski, S. G., and Demeulemeester, J. M. (2018). The BRICS Coming of Age and the New Development Bank. *Global Policy*, vol. 9, no. 4, pp. 578–585.

SWIFT. (2015, July 29). Renminbi adoption is on the rise in South Africa. www.swift.com/news-events/press-releases/renminbi-adoption-rise-south-africa

SWIFT. (2016). CIPS Accelerates the Internationalization of the RMB. *MI Forum Magazine by SWIFT*. www.swift.com/news-events/news/cips-acceler ates-internationalisation-rmb.

Taggart, G. (2011, December 23). BRICS Stock Exchanges Plan an Alliance. *Institutional Investor*.

TASS Russian News Agency. (2016, April 19). Швецов: создание единого рынка капитала в БРИКС возможно через 5 лет (Shvetsov: creation of a single capital market in BRICS is possible in 5 years). *TASS Russian News Agency*. https://tass.ru/ekonomika/3217397.

TASS Russian News Agency. (2017, November 24). BRICS Countries Mulling Formation of Single Gold Trade System. *TASS Russian News Agency*. https://tass.com/economy/977276.

TASS Russian News Agency. (2018, May 8). Putin Urges to Strengthen National Economic Sovereignty. https://tass.com/economy/1003387.

TASS Russian News Agency. (2019, June 5). Russia, China to Sign Agreement on Payments in National Currencies, Says Decree. https://tass.com/economy/1061848.

TASS Russian News Agency. (2021a, April 16). SCO Working on Gradual Transition to National Currencies in Payments. https://tass.com/economy/1279039.

TASS Russian News Agency. (2021b, June 5). Russia Does Not Want to Give Up Dollar as Reserve Currency or Means of Payment – Putin. https://tass.com/economy/1299253

Thygesen, N. et al. (1995) *International Currency Competition and the Future Role of the Single European Currency, Final Report of a Working Group on European Monetary Union – International Monetary System*. London: Kluwer Law International.

Tierney, M. J. (2014). Rising Powers and the Regime for Development Finance, *International Studies Review*, vol. 16, no. 3, pp. 452–455.

Tobor, N. (2018, June 27). South African Reserve Bank's Blockchain Project. https://iafrikan.com/2018/06/27/south-african-reserve-bank-block-chain-project/.

UN General Assembly. (2009). Experts Propose New International Reserve System as Part of Efforts to Create More Effective, Democratic Global Structures. United Nations, GA/10816-ECO/146.

UnionPay Market News. (2019, *August 23)*. UnionPay Cards Accepted at All Pick n Pay Stores across South Africa. www.unionpayintl.com/en/mediaCenter/newsCenter/marketUpdate/5514.shtml

UnionPay Media Reports. (2019, September 27). UnionPay Banks on its Innovation to Up Global Influence. www.unionpayintl.com/en/mediaCenter/newsCenter/mediaReports/5752.shtml

UnionPay International. (2021, March 18). UnionPay Acceptance Network Expands to 180 Countries and Regions, PRNewswire. www.unionpayintl.com/en/mediaCenter/newsCenter/companyNews/7374.shtml

Vnesheconombank. (2018, July 26). Vnesheconombank and BRICS Development Banks Will Research the Implementation of Blockchain Technology, *PRNewswire*.

Vorobyova, T. (2009, June 17). Russia, China to Boost Ruble, Yuan Use in Trade. *Reuters*.

Washington Post. (2011, January 16). China's Hu Jintao Answers Questions with Washington Post. www.washingtonpost.com/business/economy/chinas-hu-jintao-answers-questions-with-washington-post/2011/01/16/ABGq3NJ_story.html

Wheatley, A. (2013). *Power of Currencies and Currencies of Power*. Abingdon: Routledge for the International Institute for Strategic Studies.

Wu, X., and Wu, G. (2014). New White Plan or New Keynes Plan- How to Build a Stable and Effective International Monetary System ("新怀特计划"还是"新凯恩斯计划" – – 如何构建稳定与有效的国际货币体系). *Exploration and Free Views* (探索与争鸣), vol. 8, pp. 59–62.

Wyplosz, C. (1999). An International Role for the Euro?, in J. Dermine and P. Hillion (eds.), *European Capital Markets with a Single Currency*, Oxford: Oxford University Press, pp. 76–104.

Xiang, S. (2014). Analyzing Global Imbalance and the Global Financial Crisis from the Perspective of Global Currencies (从国际货币角度看全球失衡和金融危机). *Popular Financing* (大众理财顾问), vol. 11, pp. 22–23.

Xinhua. (2017, June 21). China to Launch 2nd Phase of Cross-Border Interbank Payment System for RMB. www.xinhuanet.com//english/2017-06/21/c_136384061.htm

Xinhua. (2009, March 31). Russia, China hold Similar Positions on Financial Reform. www.chinadaily.com.cn/china/g20/2009-03/31/content_7633245.htm

Xinhua. (2019, December 13). S. African Bank Launches UnionPay Card for Prompt Payment In. www.xinhuanet.com/english/africa/2019-12/13/c_138627709.htm

Xinhua. (2020, December 1). SCO Plans to Enhance Financial Cooperation, Continue Consultations on Establishing SCO Development Bank. www.xinhuanet.com/english/2020-12/01/c_139555549.htm

Xu, W. (2020). The SWIFT System: A Focus on the US–Russia Financial Confrontation. *Russian International Affairs Council*.

Wang, X. (2009, June 16). BRIC Summit may Focus on Reducing Dollar Dependence. *China Daily*.

Yeung, K. (2021, April 3). Could US Sanctions and closer Middle East Ties Fuel the Rise of China's Petroyuan? *South China Morning Post*.

Zhou X. (2009). Reform the International Monetary System, March 23, 2009. www.bis.org/review/r090402c.pdf.

Acknowledgments

The authors would like to thank the editor and the reviewers for their constructive feedback. We thank Kelly Sims Gallagher, Frank O'Donnell, Zhen Han, Emily Kennelly, Cameron Thies, Zihao Liu, Daniel Stemp, Ravi Shankar Chaturvedi, Rosemary Spracklin, Oleksandra Poliakova, Christopher Shim, Eleanor Hume, and Jeremy Holt for valuable input on prior drafts and the grant agency for making this work possible. This work relates to the Office of the Secretary of Defense Minerva Initiative through the Department of Navy award [N000141812744] issued by the Office of Naval Research. The United States Government has a royalty-free license throughout the world in all copyrightable materials contained herein. Any opinions, findings, and conclusions or recommendations expressed in this material are those of the author(s) and do not necessarily reflect the views of the Office of Naval Research.

Cambridge Elements ≡

Economics of Emerging Markets

Bruno S. Sergi
Harvard University

Editor Bruno S. Sergi is an instructor at Harvard University, an associate of the Harvard University Davis Center for Russian and Eurasian Studies and Harvard Ukrainian Research Institute. He is the Academic Series Editor of the Cambridge *Elements in the Economics of Emerging Markets* (Cambridge University Press), a co-editor of the *Lab for Entrepreneurship and Development* book series, and associate editor of *The American Economist*. Concurrently, he teaches International Economics at the University of Messina, Scientific Director of the Lab for Entrepreneurship and Development (LEAD), and a co-founder and Scientific Director of the International Center for Emerging Markets Research at RUDN University in Moscow. He has published over 150 articles in professional journals and 21 books as author, co-author, editor, and co-editor.

About the Series

The aim of this Elements series is to deliver state-of-the-art, comprehensive coverage of the knowledge developed to date, including the dynamics and prospects of these economies, focusing on emerging markets' economics, finance, banking, technology advances, trade, demographic challenges, and their economic relations with the rest of the world, as well as the causal factors and limits of economic policy in these markets.

Cambridge Elements $\overline{\overline{}}$

Economics of Emerging Markets

Elements in the Series

A full series listing is available at: www.cambridge.org/EEM